1998

Escaping the Advice Trap

Escaping the Advice Trap

59 Tough Relationship Problems Solved by the Experts

WENDY M. WILLIAMS, PH.D.,
AND STEPHEN J. CECI, PH.D.

Andrews McMeel Publishing

Kansas City

www.andrewsmcmeel.com

98 99 00 01 02   RDH   10 9 8 7 6 5 4 3 2 1

Library of Congress Cataloging-in-Publication Data

Williams, Wendy M. (Wendy Melissa), 1960-
   Escaping the advice trap : 59 tough relationship problems solved by the experts / by Wendy M. Williams and Stephen J. Ceci.
      p. cm.
   ISBN 0-8362-5215-2 (hardcover)
   1. Interpersonal conflict. 2. Interpersonal relations.
I. Ceci, Stephen J.   II. Title.
BF637.I48W55 1998
158.2'4—dc21   97-38193
                                          CIP

*To our friends and colleagues
who contributed their wisdom to this book*

Preface

Nobody can give you wiser advice than yourself.
—Cicero

A FRIEND RECENTLY called us for advice on a dilemma in his personal life. The problem involved Doug's daughter and his new girlfriend. Doug's situation is common today: He is a forty-five-year-old, recently divorced father with one child, a ten-year-old daughter named Ashley. Several months ago he met a woman, Meg, and started dating her regularly. She is the first woman he has dated since his divorce. In fact, before meeting Meg several weeks ago, Ashley had never seen her father with a woman other than Ashley's mother.

Doug's problem was with the upcoming holiday season. He planned to spend time with Meg, and he wanted to bring Ashley for an overnight visit to Meg's house. The way he saw it, sooner or later, Meg and Ashley had to get to know one another. But Doug was torturing himself over one issue in particular: sleeping arrangements. He had lots of questions: Should he and Meg sleep together? Should they allow Ashley to see them sharing a bed? Or should they sleep in separate rooms? Should he talk to Ashley about the situation? That's why Doug called us; he figured we were experts in the area of child development, so we should be able to advise him.

We are both psychologists who study children, and we are faculty members at Cornell University. We have written books and articles about children. We spend most of our professional time trying to understand the right way to raise healthy, well-adjusted, smart kids. We consult for numerous organizations, and we hold major grants. So Doug's idea of asking us how to handle his problem made perfect sense. He was tormenting himself trying to figure out what to do, and if we didn't know, whom could he ask?

We talked to Doug independently and gave him our best advice. We both felt good about what we had said and believed that our advice was on target. That evening we met for dinner, and Doug's situation came up. Each of us was interested to hear the other's take on Doug's problem—but it never occurred to us that our opinions differed! What advice had we given Doug?

One of us told Doug that he had nothing to worry about and that he was magnifying the problem: He should simply act naturally in front of Meg and Ashley, showing affection as he saw fit, and sleep with Meg. After all, this is the late 1990s, and children are accustomed to seeing and hearing about "reconstituted" families in the media, from friends, and everywhere else. There is a danger in shielding children from adult romantic relationships; overprotected kids grow up with unrealistic and even unhealthy images of adult sexuality. Plus, if Doug ignored his own and Meg's needs by sleeping separately, this could cause resentment to brew between Meg and Ashley and also between Meg and Doug. Meg needed to be reassured that the fact that Doug was married for many years and has a child does not mean Meg will get the short end of the stick.

The other one of us told Doug that he was wise to worry about sleeping with Meg with Ashley in the house. As an only child of the opposite sex, she was likely to become jealous of his affection for "another woman." This jealousy could cause major troubles down the road for the relationships between Doug and Meg and between Doug and Ashley. Given that Meg might not last as Doug's main love interest, he would be exposing his daughter to a woman who might not be a permanent part of her life. The result? Ashley could get the idea that adult love relationships are short-lived and disposable. If Ashley came to like Meg, she might be crushed when Meg disappeared from the scene. Or, if Ashley disliked Meg, Ashley's behavior might be blamed for the failure of the adult relationship.

When we compared the advice we had given Doug, we were surprised. We assumed that experts in a field, both of whom had a friend's best interest at heart, and both of whom knew the same details about the situation, would see things similarly and base their answers on the same scientific evidence. In fact, both of us had drawn on scientific research; we'd just focused on different findings. Or, worse yet, we'd interpreted the same findings differently when we applied them to Doug's case. We wondered aloud how Doug must have felt after hearing opposing advice from his two expert friends!

The next day we called Doug and asked him. He said our opinions both perplexed and liberated him. When he realized experts differed in their opinions, he knew he was not being forced to see the one "correct" way to handle the situation. He also said we had agreed about some aspects of his problem, so he knew these were the important points to focus on. For instance, we had both stressed how things would seem from Ashley's point of view versus Meg's, and we had both noted that a ten-year-old cannot be expected to reason like an adult. So, when Doug sat down to mull over his decision that night, he knew how to analyze the situation, focus on what really mattered, and come up with the right answer for him.

Our experience with Doug showed us two important things about getting advice from experts. First, we were reminded that even well-intentioned, well-credentialed professionals often disagree when it comes to practical, everyday problems with families and relationships. The trouble is that most people don't realize this. Most people are willing to take advice from a single expert—a psychotherapist, talk-show host, advice columnist, religious adviser, or whomever—without considering alternative opinions. The average person listens to the first "expert's" opinion and believes it. Often, this opinion affects fundamental, life-altering decisions about relationships, work, and child rearing: People file for divorce on the basis of a single marriage counselor's opinion, change jobs on the basis of a single occupational adviser's analysis, and raise their kids the way a single psychologist tells them to.

Imagine the same people confronted with a medical crisis. If told they need open-heart surgery, the same individuals would immediately seek a second—and third—opinion! If told they have breast cancer, these people would immediately consult other physicians. But when it comes to psychological problems, people are more gullible. In the psychological domain, our society encourages ready reliance upon "experts"— just turn on the television or radio, and you will find an expert willing to solve your problems on the spot. Often all you have to do is dial a 900 telephone number and pay five bucks a minute. Nowhere are you informed that experts sometimes disagree and that before changing your life on the basis of an expert's advice you should get a second opinion—preferably an opinion from the opposite perspective.

The second important lesson we learned from our experience with Doug was that, despite the fact that experts may disagree on specifically what to do, they often agree on the most important factors in the situation. These are the factors that should be considered carefully during decision making. Experts have thought about the problems enough to know what these key issues are. They may not see the same way when it comes to a desirable outcome, but they do see the same key points to consider. What this means is that by hearing the differing opinions of experts, people can focus their thinking to arrive at optimal solutions for them.

This book gives you insights developed from listening to experts who sometimes disagree. By reading it you will gain the knowledge and confidence to consider expert opinions and then solve relationship problems your own way. This book shows that sometimes even the most recognized experts in a field disagree on all types of problems faced in relationships and families. We present fifty-nine problems typical of the perplexing, real-world situations that come up in all our lives, followed by the answers of two or more experts. Finally, we discuss the professionals' areas of agreement and disagreement and give a "bottom-line" analysis.

Unlike most self-help manuals, which provide a single expert's opinion on a wide range of problems, our book recognizes that genuine expertise is far more limited. Most books and advice columns begin and end with a single expert, who answers all the questions. This book began with a list of real-world problems, for which we chose appropriate expert commentators. This book features over one hundred professionals, each commenting on one or more problems on the topics they know best.

Not every problem in this book will be relevant to every reader. However, one thing is certain: Readers will find all the problems and answers intriguing! The message in these pages is clear: *Caveat lector* (reader beware). Just because a person is an expert doesn't mean that his or her advice is right for you, or that a second expert wouldn't give you the opposite opinion. Ultimately, when it comes to family and relationship problems, we would all be more successful if we used experts to help focus our thinking, instead of allowing individual experts' opinions to run our lives. The best decisions are the ones we make for ourselves, after learning how to think like experts about a problem. As Cicero said: "Nobody can give you wiser advice than yourself."

You can't have your Kate and Edith, too.
—Country-western song

My boyfriend and I broke up. He wanted to get married, and I didn't want him to.
—Rita Rudner

Problem 1

MY BEST FRIEND HAS BEEN DATING a woman for the past eighteen months, and they have an understanding that neither of them dates anyone else. Recently, however, an old female friend of his suggested that they meet for dinner when she comes to town. Although he and this woman never dated, he always felt attracted to her when she lived in town. He feels totally torn; part of him wants to pursue the possibilities that this could create, yet part of him wonders whether he is ethically bound to honor his current lover's trust in him. When he asked me what I thought, I found myself wavering between the view that he had a right (perhaps even a responsibility) to investigate this new relationship, inasmuch as he himself states that he is not completely sure of his feelings for his current lover. However, I wonder if "the grass is always greener" with a new lover. (I should add that my friend is a divorced forty-four-year-old.)

PROFESSIONAL OPINIONS

John Paul Gray, Ph.D., Clinical Psychologist, San Juan Capistrano, CA;
Past President, Orange County Psychological Association
➤ If this were my friend, I'd say to him, "Stop playing games in your head. If you have a commitment with this woman, you

are bound to honor it. If the commitment doesn't fit anymore, be courageous enough to tell your girlfriend (a woman, incidentally, who deserves your respect) that you need to redefine 'dating.' Be a man about it or start identifying yourself as a weasel.

"But your real problem sounds like you need to back off your eighteen-month relationship and that you're using your fantasies about the old friend as a catalyst. People do that, it's true, but we should try to learn better. Part of learning better is keeping the issues straight and not blaming your girlfriend for your ambivalences. Like that 'trust' thing. It's not something you 'owe' your girlfriend; it's something within you that reflects your character and your personal code of living. Get straight with yourself first.

"Love is a powerful thing. When two people are committed in a relationship, there can be a lot of tolerance for divergent activities done separately; independent activities can enrich the relationship. Mature people (regardless of age) value and protect their relationships because they give something really important back. And that's an emotional, and sometimes spiritual, home. But, frankly, it doesn't sound like you're there. Remember, the most alluring woman in the world can't seduce you if you're not seducible, and you are in charge of that. Love is that powerful. Your job is to take a stand on your priorities."

George Levinger, Ph.D., Author, Editor, Researcher, and Professor Emeritus, University of Massachusetts; Recipient of the 1990 Distinguished Career Contribution Award from the International Society for the Study of Personal Relationships

➤ I see two important aspects in your friend's question. The first is the meaning of honesty in a close relationship; the second concerns how to recognize and deal with strains in his existing relationship. Regarding honesty, I think that breaking any clear understanding is an act of infidelity. But the mere act of going out to dinner with the out-of-town woman need not be such a breach, unless your friend tries to keep it a secret. It seems appropriate for him to tell his lover that he intends to meet an old acquaintance for dinner when she comes to town, and even to suggest that the three of them get together afterward. If his partner seems jealous or offended, there may be tensions in their current connection that he should discuss with her.

Regarding such strains, you should talk with your friend about the danger signals in his question to you and his feeling "totally torn" about the possibilities this meeting could create. What is the meaning of his worries? Is he actually thinking of breaking up his present relationship or not? If your friend were indeed to find that he is more attracted to the second woman than to his present partner—and it's possible he will imagine that "the grass is greener" elsewhere—this would become a new issue. However, there are reasons why this is unlikely after his not having seen the old acquaintance for so long.

Altogether, I see no necessity for your friend either to deceive his partner or to deprive himself of seeing an old acquaintance. I do, however, believe that he should honestly deal with his feelings toward his partner and with hers toward him.

BOTTOM LINE

➤ Both experts agree that it is important in this situation for the man to ask himself why he is staying with a woman he's been dating for eighteen months if, by his own admission, he is unsure of his feelings for her, and if he is actively attracted to other women. Perhaps he is ambivalent about committing to anyone following his divorce. Perhaps he is looking for an excuse to move on and sample another woman's wares. Perhaps he doesn't really want to be in an exclusive relationship, but he is also afraid to spend his evenings alone. Thus, he may be staying with his girlfriend out of dependency and loneliness instead of love.

In any case, both experts agree that weaseling around behind his girlfriend's back is not the answer. This man should be honest about it if he plans to see the woman from his past. After all, a simple dinner with an old friend should not be a big deal, unless there are major problems and insecurities in a relationship. And if there are such problems, a productive discussion might ensue following the man's announcement that he plans to see an old female friend for dinner. This man must ask himself if he is being completely honest and fair with his girlfriend—as well as with himself. Anyone who considers himself this fellow's best friend should advise him to ask these questions.

Sometimes when a person has been in a relationship for a while, the grass looks lusher and greener elsewhere. Most people recognize that lack of familiarity with the outsider creates a rosier-than-reality mental picture of a hypothetical relationship with this individual. But some people don't. A woman who's been dating a guy for eighteen months has a right to know if he's sniffing around, and if so whether he intends to do more than just sniff. An open discussion should illuminate the landscape for this woman.

[What do women want?] Exactly what men want: love, money, excitement, pleasure, happiness, fulfilling work—and sometimes a child who will say, "I love you."
　　　—Dr. Joyce Brothers

You know the problem with men? After the birth, we're irrelevant.
　　　—Dustin Hoffman

Problem 2

SEVEN YEARS AGO, when I met my future husband, we discussed having children, and we agreed that we wanted to have two kids once we were financially secure. I am now thirty-seven, and although our financial situation is not ideal, it is not bad either. But my husband says we simply aren't ready or stable enough financially to begin a family. I am getting more and more worried, because I know that my chances of becoming pregnant are dropping dramatically as I approach forty. I want children very much, and I always have. I made these feelings completely clear to my husband before we married, and now I feel that he is breaking his promise to have a family with me. What should I do?

PROFESSIONAL OPINIONS

Sandra Bem, Ph.D., Author, Editor, Researcher, and Professor, Cornell University

Given your age, I think the two of you have to move beyond your husband's argument that, as a couple, you aren't financially ready to have children. The phrase "financially ready" implies that having children is only a matter of time, but time is so short for you biologically that waiting for further financial security would not seem to be a viable option. Perhaps just making this clearer to your husband will bring him around. But if not, you need to communicate as lovingly and decisively as possible that the discussion must henceforth explore other issues that might be under the surface. For example, if readiness is an issue at all, perhaps it's a matter of your husband's psychological readiness, in which case he could work on that during your pregnancy. Or perhaps he doesn't really want children after all. Or perhaps he isn't even committed enough to the marriage to tie himself more tightly to it by having children.

As upsetting as these possibilities may be, they and others need to be put on the table and openly discussed or you'll never get anywhere. You also need to think through and discuss your own feelings about staying in the relationship if you can't have children. For example, how much irreparable damage will be done to the relationship if your husband denies you children? Are you willing to consider ending the marriage if children are ruled out? Are you willing (and financially able) to raise children on your own if the marriage breaks up? These are all terribly difficult issues to consider, but discussing them may be the only way for the two of you to clarify what really is and is not important to you.

Laurence Steinberg, Ph.D., Author, Editor, Researcher, and Professor, Temple University

➤ Bringing a child into the world in the midst of minor financial problems is not insurmountable, but starting a family without the support and cooperation of your spouse is a potential nightmare. You two need to talk. I would leave aside the issue of who promised what when you were courting—people change over time, and marriages need to be flexible. Instead of focusing on the past, talk about your present feelings. It's important for the two of you to have a candid discussion about the situation and determine whether finances are really the issue. If they are, see if you can define the issue as one that could benefit from collaborative problem solving. Sit down with your husband and discuss, in concrete terms, what sort of financial security is necessary for the two of you to feel comfortable with the idea of starting a family. With real numbers in front of you (e.g., how much things cost, how much you have saved, what sorts of changes you will have to make in your lifestyle), you should be able to come up with a plan that suits both of you. If, however, finances aren't the problem, you may want to schedule an appointment with a counselor to talk things out.

BOTTOM LINE

～The wife in this situation is beginning to get the picture that "financial security" isn't the whole story—and both experts raise the possibility that she may be right. The issue of finances seems more like a convenient excuse to delay childbearing. Thus, it is essential that the wife confront her husband with this possibility and encourage him to speak to the point: What is he really afraid of? If the husband simply cannot envision himself wanting or raising children, the wife has three options: (1) leave him and become pregnant on her own, via artificial insemination or other means; (2) stay in the relationship and try to become pregnant "by accident" with her husband, in the hope that once he sees his biological issue he won't regret having a child; or (3) stay in the relationship and accept that she will be childless unless he has a (very unlikely) change of heart.

One thing is clear: Time's a'wastin'. The woman must move forward immediately, given the declining fertility statistics for her age-group. She must ask herself if life without children will be complete. If the answer is no, she must ask herself whether her husband would come around once he held his own child. If the answer is again no, or if she is unsure of the answer, she must leave and pursue other options. It might be preferable to leave and wind up childless after trying to conceive, for example, rather than stay and be eaten away with resentment—which would ultimately destroy the relationship anyway. The key is that she must decide now, based on the evidence at hand. There will never be perfect and complete information from which to draw conclusions in a situation like this one. The bottom line is that waiting is simply not an option: She has already waited too long.

Without love, intelligence is dangerous;
without intelligence, love is not enough.
　　—Ashley Montagu

The highest result of education is tolerance.
　　—Helen Keller

Cauliflower is nothing but a cabbage with a college education.
　　—Mark Twain

I never let schooling interfere with my education.
　　—Mark Twain

Problem 3

I AM A THIRTY-YEAR-OLD MAN who has been dating a thirty-two-year-old woman for three years. I care for this woman very much, but she is from a working-class family, whereas I am from an upper-middle-class family. She is uneducated, she does not speak grammatically, and in general she does not show the signs of a solid education that is so valued in my family. Last week this woman's father gave us an ultimatum: Either we get married by Christmas or she must break up with me. The trouble is, I do not feel ready for marriage! But I do not want to lose her either, and I have to make a choice. I keep thinking that there are too many reasons we don't belong together, but at the same time I must admit that I care for her very much and would be crushed if she left me. Should I marry her, or lose her and risk being alone and not finding anyone else I care for as much?

PROFESSIONAL OPINIONS

Melanie Anson, Ph.D., Author and Instructor, Citrus College

🔺 It is my opinion, through experience, that after three years one should be ready to make a rational and emotional decision to be with a person in a marriage or mutually agreeable partnership. This man is not really interested in being with this woman except for convenience, because her grammatical errors and socioeconomic level still visibly disturb him. Thus, it is only fair to her to let her go free. Her father is right. This man needs to find someone he can be proud of, not try to mold this woman into something for his own needs. . . . It would never work out ultimately.

Douglas P. Peters, Ph.D., Author, Editor, Researcher, and Professor,
University of North Dakota

🔺 You're only thirty years old, and in many ways, this is not that old for a man today. Thus, your reluctance regarding marriage is understandable. It is normal to be wary of a lifelong commitment. You state that you care for this woman very much, and indeed the possibility of being without her upsets you. It sounds to me like you are looking for an excuse to buy more time and avoid making a commitment now. However, her father is understandably concerned about the length of time you and his daughter have been dating, and about her increasing age and decreasing marriageability.

In my opinion, the problems you mention are soluble: She could attend college for two years, improve her level of education and use of English, and generally become more acceptable to your family. But why does the approval of your family matter this much? If she is a good, kind, honest person, that should matter far more than the perfect use of English. Perhaps you should think through what qualities will matter the most to you in the long run in a partnership. My advice is to encourage this woman to better herself, with your support, and make a commitment to her. Perhaps you are no day at the beach! If you are simply unwilling to commit, you should let her go; however, my take is that you really want to stay with her but are experiencing natural feelings of fear at the thought of marriage.

David F. Ross, Ph.D., Author, Editor, Researcher, and Assistant Professor, University of Tennessee

━I don't care if she is formally educated—that should be irrelevant to the decision to continue in the relationship. What is education anyway? Some of the most financially successful people I know (three or four of whom are self-made multimillionaires) have no formal education, but they are vastly educated (far more than most of the Ph.D.'s I know) in the workings of the real world. I think this young couple should tell the father to go to hell. She is thirty-two, not fifteen years of age: What right does her father have to make an ultimatum like that? If she doesn't have the guts to stand up to her father, I think this man should leave her because she isn't right for him. If I were this guy, I would want a woman who is an independent entity irrespective of her educational level. I hate families who meddle in the lives of their grown children, and for a couple to acquiesce to the woman's father is disgusting.

BOTTOM LINE

━The experts' analyses lead them to vastly different conclusions, from "her father is right" to "tell the father to go to hell." The bottom line is that this man must make a decision: His girlfriend deserves nothing less. If he cannot make a commitment to her at this time, for whatever reason, he must cut her loose. She wants to marry, and he should not tie her up for years while making up his mind. What if he never feels ready? It could be that this man is perennially a boy who does not want to become tied down. If so, being forced into a marriage will be the worst possible thing for him, and for his girlfriend.

The key is that he must make a decision. The fact that he is so reluctant suggests that she is not the right woman for him. Either that, or no woman would be, because he is not ready. Often people who feel unready later find themselves feeling differently in a relationship with someone else. No one should force himself to marry. The woman's father has a right to expect a decision, and this man must make one. If he cannot welcome this woman into his life with happiness and an earnest desire to share, he should set her free.

Angels we have heard on high,
tell us to go out and buy.
—Tom Lehrer

Riches are for spending.
—Francis Bacon

'Tis better than riches to scratch when it itches.
—Anon.

With money in your pocket, you are wise and you
are handsome, and you sing well too.
—Jewish proverb

Problem 4

MY TWENTY-EIGHT-YEAR-OLD husband and I have different priorities for how to spend money. He is impulsive and enjoys buying things on the spot—flowers for me, an expensive jacket for him, gifts for our children, you name it. He always pays our credit cards in full every month, and we are not in debt. I, however, would like to save to buy a home (we now rent), and more generally I would like to save for the future. Meanwhile, my husband goes on planning expensive and romantic vacations! I have told my husband how I feel, and especially that I believe that it is important to provide our children with stability for the future, but all he says is that we could be dead in a year and it is important to "live for the moment"! It worries me to think that our lives will never be materially secure. What should I do?

PROFESSIONAL OPINIONS

Keith Dobson, Ph.D., Author, Researcher, and Professor, University of Calgary; Past President, Canadian Psychological Association

➤ It is obvious that you and your husband share the virtue of being responsible persons, but you apparently take a longer view of things than he does. I also get the sense that you may not have been able to effectively tell him your concerns about the lack of future financial planning. I worry a bit that his impulsive buying may not be fully under his control. I think that you should review how you express your worries to your husband and develop an effective strategy to speak to him. Try to pick a time and a way that he will hear you, and propose a plan that both he and you can live with. If he still will not listen, then you may have to be more forceful in what you say. It is possible that you may need to help him learn to control his impulses, for example by telling him that you would rather he not plan impulsive vacations but put that money into savings. If these ideas do not help, you may need to reevaluate how committed he is to really working with you.

Kelly D. Brownell, Ph.D., Author, Editor, Researcher, and Professor, Yale University; Past President, Division of Health Psychology, American Psychological Association

➤ There is no substitute for communication and problem solving. The first step is for you and your husband to speak openly, about both the money issues and the feelings unleashed by your different approaches. Then the problem solving can begin. The spontaneity your husband displays is often done with a sense of good fun and kindness to others, so why stifle it? Still, you and he might find ways for him to retain this nice part of his personality while spending less money. Vacations need not be expensive to be romantic, so perhaps he could challenge himself to find creative, low-cost excursions. With gifts, he might remind himself that the thought counts most, so less expensive but spontaneous gift giving can still feel rewarding for all involved.

Nuran Hortaqsu, Ph.D., Author and Professor, Middle East Technical University

〜 I think you and your husband should each begin by making a list of the things you want to do in the near and farther future together, with realistic costs of each item. In addition, each of you should give priority ratings for each item. You should then sit down and try to make plans so that each of you can achieve what he or she most desires, either by more efficient use of your resources (economizing here and there) or by some compromise in which one gives up a lower-priority item for the sake of an item that has high priority for the other. For example, during your discussions about efficient ways of handling finances, you might be able to persuade your husband that investing in a home you sell later on might provide the resources for a holiday that you could not afford while you pay rent. You might also try discussing your general orientations with respect to living in the present versus the future and coming to a compromise. By the way, I want to remind you that you will not be in your twenties for long. Romantic holidays might not feel as romantic when you are fifty.

David F. Ross, Ph.D., Author, Editor, Researcher, and Assistant Professor, University of Tennessee

〜 My suggestion to the wife is to change her views and go spend money with her husband. He sounds like a fun guy: Romantic vacations, flowers—this guy is a winner! Who wants a relationship with a stick-in-the-mud? Not me! I agree with the husband: You both could be dead in a year, and if you don't have some fun, you're already dead! As Samuel Johnson said, "It's better to live rich than to die rich." The guy is not overspending—he pays off the credit card debt every month.

If you want a house, go out and get a job and start saving for one. I say go have some fun and spend the money. Too many people wait for life to start when they retire after saving for their entire lives. But then they find it's too late—so start living now!

George Levinger, Ph.D., Author, Editor, Researcher, and Professor Emeritus, University of Massachusetts; Recipient of the 1990 Distinguished Career Contribution Award from the International Society for the Study of Personal Relationships

～ I would guess that you and your husband have had very different experiences with money while growing up. In order to find a healthy solution to your disagreement, it would be helpful to explore the bases of your different orientations to money. The fact that you are not in debt, and that your husband regularly pays off your credit card bills, shows that he has his spending under some control. On that basis, it seems possible to negotiate an agreement that satisfies both of your needs: his for spontaneity and yours for security. For example, the two of you might agree to have a set amount of money deducted from each paycheck to go into savings while still allowing spontaneity in spending on fun adventures. If you cannot arrive at such a solution by yourselves, you might seek the assistance of someone else you both respect. Ideally, your husband will better understand that his desire to live for the moment does not have to make you anxious and insecure, while you will become more appreciative of his longing for frivolity and romance.

BOTTOM LINE

～ Four of the five experts agree that some sort of compromise is called for here. Goals should be prioritized, and spending should be moderated. But one expert believes the problem is all due to the wife's lack of imagination and extreme rigidity. We believe that the bottom line is that it is completely natural to want to own a home instead of renting forever: This woman's desires are reasonable! True, this couple is young, but they are parents, and with children come greater financial responsibilities. The husband seems to have a problem with a need for instant gratification; his impulses to purchase on-the-spot presents and his generally unstoppable urge to spend demonstrate this fact. Does he have other compulsive needs—such as eating, smoking, or drinking too much? If so, he might be a good candidate for impulse-control therapy. If his main problem is spending, then he could rein in his behavior with the help of his wife. It is important to remember that this is not a serious spending problem, because the family does pay its bills on time each month. Thus, drastic measures are not called for in this situation.

First, the wife must make her feelings clear to her husband: She must state how upset she becomes when no savings are set aside and no house seems in the works. She should also tell her husband that she worries about how well the family can weather future financial crises with no cash reserves. The husband needs some discretionary money that he can spend without his wife's approval, but not so much money that the couple never saves for the future. Perhaps together, they can draw up a budget and the husband can pledge to stick to it, to get his wife's approval for all purchases over a certain amount, and to spend no more than his discretionary money on frivolous items. With regard to vacations, perhaps the couple can choose less expensive locations closer to home, rather than far-away spots that are more expensive. A couple of guidebooks might help the husband see that there are often many fun and interesting things to do and places to see closer to home and for less money than he is used to spending.

Adopted kids are such a pain—you have
to teach them to look like you.
    —Gilda Radner

Make yourself necessary to somebody.
    —Ralph Waldo Emerson

The great use of life is to spend it for something that will outlast it.
    —William James

Problem 5

MY HUSBAND AND I have been trying to conceive a child for six years. We've been through fertility treatments but so far have had no luck. I think it is time to adopt a child—any healthy child—but my husband says he is not interested in raising "someone else's" child and only wants a child if it is his own. He seems truly anxious to become a father, but he does not understand that we could love an adopted child just as much as if it were our own. We are both in our midthirties. What should I do?

PROFESSIONAL OPINIONS

Lynne M. Webb, Ph.D., Author, Researcher, and Associate Professor,
University of Memphis; Past President, Southern States Communication
Association

If you adopt a child and your husband subsequently fails to accept the child as his own, the situation will be disastrous for all involved. Therefore, you both should explore thoroughly your feelings about adoption. Several avenues exist for such exploration: (1) Begin the home study that all reputable adoption agencies require. You can discuss your feelings with an experienced, trained professional during the required six counseling sessions. Afterward, most couples decide to proceed with adoption, but many do not. (2) Attend support group meetings for adoptive parents; prospective adoptive parents routinely attend such meetings to talk out concerns. Listen to the problems adoptive families face; decide if you can handle them. (3) Spend some extended time caring for children. Arrange to baby-sit one child for an entire weekend; volunteer in your church or temple's nursery; coach a Little League team. You will discover that you do or do not grow attached to children regardless of their parentage. (4) Examine the wealth of books and articles about adoption. Many authors discuss the feelings you describe as well as additional important topics. After this exploration, you each will know whether you are open to adoption; proceed with a joint adoption only if you both desire it.

Irving Tallman, Ph.D., Author, Researcher, and Professor,
Washington State University

➤ Before you decide what to do, you should ask yourself: If you had to make a choice, what is more important—your relationship with your husband or adopting a child? If you decide it is your relationship, then the decision you make must result from a shared commitment. This requires a frank expression and exploration of the feelings you both have and a willingness on both your parts to accept the feelings of the other partner as real and important. You should not approach this as an argument in which you hope to get your way. Rather, it is an attempt to mutually arrive at a decision that, considering the concerns of both partners, will be best for the marriage in the long run.

If you believe that having a child is as important as or more important than your relationship, then you should try to persuade your husband through reasoning, tears, or threats that adoption is the only acceptable solution for you. If he accepts your solution, you may eventually have to deal with his resentment about having been pressured or cajoled into a situation he did not want.

BOTTOM LINE

⬳ Both of the experts agree that the bottom line is that this woman must decide how badly she wants to adopt. If, on the one hand, she wants to adopt but is not wedded to the idea, then she should try to persuade and educate her husband. If this succeeds, they can pursue the adoption idea further. If he doesn't budge, she can forget about it. If, on the other hand, she decides that her life would simply not be complete without a child, she can try more strenuously to move her husband in the direction of adoption. If he is completely against the idea, her only option would be to leave him and pursue an adoption, perhaps of an older child in need of a loving home (since she may have trouble being selected to adopt a baby as a single parent), on her own.

As each expert warns, what this woman should *not* do is force her husband—he will resent her, and the child will ultimately pay the price. What she should do is let her husband know (if this is indeed the case) that the issue of becoming a parent is a deal breaker in their marriage. If he knows how much this means to her and still balks, he would have made a lousy father. If he is unsure, she can offer to do the bulk of the child-rearing work, or she can suggest that they pay a nanny to help so he won't be overburdened. In any case, she should be honest about both her feelings and her intentions.

*To be talented, hardworking, and clever enough to get a
promotion that requires uprooting your family, you must be
stupid enough to want it.*
        —Anon.

Success is the one unpardonable sin against one's fellows.
        —Ambrose Bierce

Problem 6

I AM A TWENTY-SIX-YEAR-OLD WOMAN who has just finished
getting my law degree, and I am now ready to begin looking
for a position in a firm. My professors have encouraged me to
shoot high and have told me I have great potential. In fact I
am being courted by three top-notch firms in different cities.
The problem is my husband. First of all, he prefers to live in a
small town, and second, he believes it would be wrong for the
two of us to move for my career. He works in hospital adminis-
tration, and he could easily get a position in any of the cities I
am considering. But all he says is that he wants to stay put. My
prospects where we now live are limited. When we married
four years ago, I made my career intentions clear, and my husband didn't protest—but now it's a different story. What
should I do?

PROFESSIONAL OPINIONS

*Karen J. Prager, Ph.D., Family Psychologist, Author, and Professor,
University of Texas*

➤ Take a two-stage approach to your husband's objections.
First, assume that his reluctance is coming from anxiety about

the change. Listen to and acknowledge his concerns (without defending your position). Find out what aspect of the move is most disturbing to him and communicate your willingness to accommodate his needs (since he would be making the move for you). For example, if his concern is the large city atmosphere, offer to commute to work from a suburb. The idea is for both of you to have most of what you want. If this process fails, however (i.e., if he refuses to work it out with you), he is betraying your agreement and engaging you in a power struggle that you cannot win (if you give up the opportunity, you keep the relationship but lose part of yourself; if you pursue the opportunity, you lose the relationship). This is a serious breach of trust and should make you wonder if he is trustworthy. Further, he is using an ultimatum to control you, and this is unlikely to be the last one in your relationship. Your second choice, then, is to pursue the offers while letting him know how much you want him to join you. Or you could try a commuting relationship as a temporary compromise. If he still refuses to budge, the relationship is probably not worth saving.

E. James Lieberman, M.D., Author and Clinical Professor,
George Washington University

➤ You have three matters to consider. First, the memory question. Does he recall agreeing to your clear statement of career plans, and does he admit to changing that agreement? I will assume the answers are yes; otherwise we have a problem of fact, or of trust.

If he has changed his position (or if you are willing to stake the relationship on your memory being better than his), then he owes you a better justification than wanting to "stay put." He gives you and your ambitions too little respect. This augurs poorly for the relationship. He owes you a major concession if he now expects you to narrow your focus because of his inertia or changing values. You may negotiate a trade-off or quid pro quo. You may hold him to his promise, at least for a few years.

The most important issue is the quality of the relationship: love, empathy, sharing risk. You present your husband as selfish and indifferent to your feelings. If other aspects of the relationship are wonderful, you might well compromise. But you might feel hurt, angry, helpless, and depressed. You have to decide whether you have been betrayed or whether you are expecting too much; it sounds like the former, and if you don't take a strong stand now, things are not likely to improve.

BOTTOM LINE

➤ The bottom line is that, because this woman made her future intentions clear to her husband before marriage, he is now obligated to move for her career. She slaved in law school so that she could get a good job. Now she has the offers, and her husband is a wet blanket. As both experts advise, she should begin by placating him and attempting to meet his needs—for instance, by offering to allow him to choose which of the three jobs she will take, by allowing him to decide where exactly they will live, and by being willing to commute farther than he does. If, despite these many concessions, he remains a wet blanket, she should take the best job and move without him. She would ultimately resent him if she gave up these opportunities, and the relationship would dissolve in time. This woman should *not* consider giving up goals she had and made clear before marriage just because her husband is anxious or jealous of her success. If he truly loves and supports her, there are many potential compromises—for example, the couple could live in a city or suburb and purchase a small second home in the countryside with the extra money that will now be coming into the household. If her husband does not truly love her, the woman is ultimately better off without him.

When marriage is outlawed, only outlaws will have in-laws.
—Anon.

*Relations are simply a tedious pack of people who
haven't got the remotest knowledge of how to live,
nor the smallest instinct about when to die.*
—Oscar Wilde

Problem 7

I AM A MARRIED MOTHER of two kids, and the way I see it, I have a problem with my in-laws. My husband's family are decent people, but they have their own way of doing things, and it drives me crazy. They drop in on us without calling, they expect us to attend a lot of family events and get-togethers (about once a week), and they want to spend a great deal of time with us in general. About once a week, I ask my husband's mother to watch the children so that she'll have time with them. I also remember my in-laws' birthdays and buy them gifts and otherwise act like a respectful daughter-in-law. But I come from a small family, and I would rather spend time alone with my husband and kids instead of being under constant pressure to be so tight with my husband's family. How should I handle this situation?

PROFESSIONAL OPINIONS

*Barbara R. Sarason, Ph.D., Author, Editor, and Research Professor,
University of Washington*

➤ You don't mention whether you have discussed your feelings with your husband. If he feels the same way you do, you can hear his ideas about solving the problem and plan a joint strategy. If he doesn't feel the same, you can suggest some compromise concerning time spent. Do you work outside the home, making your family time limited? Are your in-laws retired with a lot of time on their hands? Do you feel they like you? Are they too bossy or prying? Perhaps you could share your feelings with your husband, not as complaints but in the context of wanting to spend more time together as a family.

Your comment about your mother-in-law getting time with the kids by baby-sitting suggests that you may be giving her a negative message about your feelings for her. Perhaps she'd feel more appreciated if sometimes you asked her to join you and the kids to do something fun. It sounds as if you are bottling up a lot of anger toward your in-laws. Communication and problem solving with your husband seems like the first step.

Catherine Stein, Ph.D., Clinical Psychologist, Researcher, and Associate Professor, Bowling Green State University

➤ First, discuss your feelings about your in-laws with your husband. Does he know you need to have family time with him and the children, rather than spending all your free moments with his parents and extended family? If he understands how you feel, perhaps you and your husband can talk with his parents about the situation. The two of you may diplomatically suggest that your in-laws pick out the three or four most important family events in the next few months that they wish you all to attend, so you will be sure to set the time aside. You may also encourage his parents to call before they visit, since you and your husband won't have time enough to spend with them if they don't call first. If your husband thinks that the frequency of his parents' visits is just fine, then you need to come to some negotiated agreement with him before approaching your in-laws. You want to avoid keeping your husband from seeing his parents. Rather, you and your husband should present a united front in helping his parents see that good relationships between adult children and their parents are based on closeness *and* separateness.

Bottom Line

～Both experts agree that the first order of business is for this woman to size up the extent of any difference of opinion between her and her husband. If she and her husband agree that they are spending too much time with his parents, they can decide on a plan of action to limit the time spent. However, if they do not agree—and if the husband feels the amount of time spent is fine—the first step is to negotiate a compromise both partners can accept. The wife should explain to her husband how she feels and remind him that these people are his relatives and not hers.

Once the partners can see eye to eye on a compromise, they must present a united front in dealing with his parents. First of all, using the grandparents as baby-sitters is not a good idea unless they explicitly ask to baby-sit. They may feel they are being treated like convenient stand-ins when the parents (and especially the mother) have something better to do. Next, the husband should sit down with his folks and inform them that his family has decided they no longer wish to have any drop-in guests, for any reason. He should not blame this new rule on his wife—he should state that it was a family decision to help the family better manage its private time. He may have to endure the cold-shoulder treatment from his parents, but if they are decent people, they will get the point. A certain number of family events should be attended, but no more than the wife can tolerate. The in-laws may feel a bit shut out, since their style of living is different from this couple's. But it is the husband and wife who must choose how they will live, and it is their right to have the amount of contact they feel is comfortable.

Another way to take on this problem is for the husband and wife to encourage his parents to take up a hobby or to travel—something that will direct their attention elsewhere and give the couple a needed break. It could be that the in-laws are lonely or have too much time on their hands. Encouraging them to expand their horizons a bit might take some pressure off of everyone.

*If I ever marry, it will be on a sudden
impulse—as a man shoots himself.*
    —H. L. Mencken

Love quickens all the senses—except common sense.
    —Anon.

Problem 8

A CLOSE FRIEND AND CO-WORKER is planning to marry a woman he hardly knows. They have been dating for less than six weeks. He says that since half of marriages end in divorce despite the fact that the couples knew each other very well before marriage, this shows that it is not necessary to know each other beforehand. He argues that the success of so-called arranged marriages is further evidence that it isn't necessary to know one's future spouse that well before getting married. He feels that it is just as easy to work out problems after you get married as it is before. Is he right or is he deluding himself?

PROFESSIONAL OPINIONS

*Cindy Hazan, Ph.D., Author, Researcher, and Associate Professor,
Cornell University*

➤ Marriage after only six weeks of dating? What, is he crazy? Your friend defends his decision by citing the high divorce rate among couples who presumably knew each other before marriage. In fact, most couples don't know each other all that well beforehand; they just think they do. And often the little they do know isn't that important. For instance, they make much of finding that they like the same movies while ignoring signs of grossly discrepant values about money. Arranged marriages are based on compatibilities of a more basic sort, and the prospective spouses usually have veto power if the chemistry isn't right. The important difference is that these matches aren't based solely on chemistry, which your friend's is likely to be. Research suggests that when people are madly in love, their brains are flooded with a natural stimulant that also acts as a mild hallucinogen. Romantic love produces a "high" that can literally blind one to danger signs and, at the same time, make the relationship feel so good and so right. In time, this effect wears off and reality sets in, which is why your friend would be wise to give it a little more time.

Benjamin R. Karney, Ph.D., Author, Researcher, and Assistant Professor, University of Florida

～ Before our friend rushes into anything, he needs to get his facts straight. Although he is right that over 50 percent of marriages end in separation or divorce, it is also true that couples who have known each other less time before marriage have higher divorce rates. Why should this be true? Couples who skip courtship have less time to experience each other in different contexts. To the extent that the partners have never coped with challenges, they may be unpleasantly surprised by each other's responses when difficult times arise in the marriage. The consequences of such surprises are much worse after marriage than before. If our friend truly loves this woman, then what's his hurry? He should enjoy his current feelings and the process of discovering this person. If the relationship continues to grow, the opportunity to marry her will still be there. But if the relationship turns out to lack the strength to endure hard times, then he will be thankful to find this out before getting married.

BOTTOM LINE

⌒ The experts agree: This man is deluding himself. What is amazing is how many people rush into major life decisions, such as marriage, guided only by their hormones and "southern brain." This man would probably spend more time picking out a new suit than he's spending on selecting a wife! In a world in which there are few absolutes, we have found one: Never marry someone you do not know well. Only after the surges of hormones have subsided does the thinking brain kick in; only after several months (or even longer) do another person's annoying habits surface. No one can stay on her or his best behavior forever, and (as wise farmers say) it is essential to size up a cow's true nature before buying it. Most couples report that traits that mildly irked them before marriage became substantial obstacles after marriage. Believe them. Sharing a preference for banana ice cream will be a distant memory as two partners are fighting over whether to spend money on vacations or save for a home. Plus, what's the rush? Even for a person who fears growing old and lonely, the alternative of growing old entrenched in battle is no better. So the bottom line is, wait and see.

Alcoholism isn't a spectator sport.
Eventually, the whole family gets to play.
—Joyce Rebeta-Burdill

It was a woman who drove me to drink—and,
you know, I never even thanked her.
—W. C. Fields

I drink to make other people interesting.
—George Jean Nathan

Problem 9

MY HUSBAND IS AN ALCOHOLIC. For several years he has fought his habit—spending a few months sober at a time while attending A.A. meetings—but alcohol always seems ultimately to win. I have had it with the verbal abuse, irresponsibility with money, and general unreliability. The trouble is that my husband is a great father! When it comes to his two sons (ages eight and ten), he is able to control himself—the anger is always unleashed alone at me. My sons adore their dad, and when he gets drunk he never lets them see him until he is recovered, so they don't understand that there is a problem. Every time I mention divorce, my husband brings our sons into the room and states, "Your mother wants Daddy to leave. What do you think about that?" Then my sons start to cry and beg me not to make their father leave. I do not know what to do. Should I stick it out?

PROFESSIONAL OPINIONS

Stevan Hobfoll, Ph.D., Author, Researcher, and Professor,
Kent State University

➤ There is no one but you who can decide if your relationship is over. However, if your husband's alcoholism, abuse, and irresponsibility have been ongoing for this long, despite treatment, they are likely to continue. At some point you have to consider your own well-being and even enjoyment of life, both for yourself and for the sake of being a good mother. It is wonderful that he has sustained a good relationship with your children, but you may need divorce counseling to preserve this relationship through a divorce, as his manipulations with the children suggest that he may continue to use them in this inappropriate way. We can hope that his positive sense of fatherhood will help him understand that using the children can and will harm them considerably. Divorce counseling can also help you both develop a good relationship as parents, even if you are no longer partners. Your guilt over the children and leaving your husband is also understandable, but if you are abused and your needs are not met, how can you be a good mother? Your sons will need your help in remaining positive about their dad, as his irresponsibility and alcoholism will inevitably weigh on them too. They and you may require therapy to emerge with positive self-esteem from this ordeal.

Christine D. MacDonald, Ph.D., Author, Researcher, and Associate
Professor, Indiana State University

➤ Definitely not. While you say that your husband is a great father, his behavior when you mention divorce is manipulative and hurtful, not only to you but also to the children. While your sons may never see their father drunk, they undoubtedly are aware that all is not well in the household—children can be very sensitive to conflict, even when adults try to conceal it from them. You are clearly miserable in this marriage, and it is difficult to be a good parent when you're miserable. Leave him. Your children are likely to be hurt less by a divorce than by staying in a household with a high level of conflict.

Jeffrey J. Haugaard, Ph.D., Clinical Psychologist, Researcher, and Associate Professor, Cornell University

～ How is it that a man who is verbally abusive, irresponsible with money, and generally unreliable is a great father? Does a good father bring his two sons into the room and demand that they take his side when you are talking about divorce? If you believe your sons do not hear your husband abusing you or see the consequences of the abuse, you are wrong. Children know what is going on at home and can hear their parents fight. It is unlikely that your children do not interact with your husband when he is drunk. Even if they do not now understand why their father acts differently at times, eventually they will see the truth.

Your husband is *not* a good father at this time. He may be a good father in the future, when he becomes sober. It is clear, however, that he cannot become sober in his current life. A separation between you and him may provide him with the motivation and new life circumstances that can facilitate sobriety. You may need the help of a counselor or therapist to explain the situation to your children. You will have to be sensitive to their needs and help them through the separation process and the ongoing interactions with their father.

Would you take your sick sons to a physician even if they did not want to go? Of course. Parents must do what is best for their children even if their children disagree. The situation with your husband will only get worse if it continues along its current course. There is no indication that it will get better. After reaching sobriety, it may be best for your husband to rejoin the family—but now it is best for all of you that he be on his own.

BOTTOM LINE

➤ All three experts urge the wife to do something drastic, such as therapy, counseling, or getting out of her marriage. The bottom line is that this woman should bite the bullet, leave her marriage, and save herself and her two children. Her husband needs help, but she cannot save him. He has tried—which is to his credit—but he has not succeeded in conquering his problem, and his wife should not sit by and allow him to control the situation. This woman appears to be confusing being a good father with simply loving one's children and being devoted to them. Her husband may love his children, but in many ways he is a dysfunctional father who represents an inappropriate role model for his sons. We agree with the experts who say that as the boys grow older, they will see more and more of the pathology in their parents' relationship, and they may suffer as a result of this pathology.

This woman needs counseling, and she might also try attending an Al-Anon group. Her children may be at risk for developing behavioral disturbances because of their early experiences as the children of an alcoholic. For these reasons, this woman should bring herself up to speed on the literature about children of alcoholics so that she can remain alert to the danger signals and be ready to help her sons develop into fully functional human beings. As for herself, she should relax and remember the three C's: She didn't *cause* the problem, she couldn't *control* it, and she can't *cure* it. She should build the best life possible for herself and her sons, a life completely free from alcohol addiction.

I'd love to kiss you but I just washed my hair.
    —Bette Davis

We wedded men live in sorrow and care.
    —Geoffrey Chaucer

Problem 10

EVERY TIME I WANT TO HAVE SEX, my wife of fifteen years says the moment just isn't right. It could be that something went wrong that day, the house isn't clean, it's too warm or too cold, or she has other things to do. The only way I can get her to relax and get in a romantic mood is to take her out to dinner, send the kids to a neighbor's, have the house perfectly clean, have candles and soft music waiting when we return home, and really romance her for a couple hours. I'm happy to do this when we have time, but real life doesn't allow this type of preparation very often! The result is that we have sex only about once a month, and this isn't nearly often enough for me. What should I do?

PROFESSIONAL OPINIONS

Robert Perloff, Ph.D., Author, Editor, Researcher, and Professor, University of Pittsburgh; Past President, American Psychological Association

Openly and honestly discuss your sexual needs with your wife, telling her that you are attracted to and in love with her in all ways, including libidinously, and that you are experiencing a void in your life because of the infrequency of sexual relations with her. At the same time, search in your mind for things that you believe she wants to do, activities that are important for her but that you don't share frequently. Show her that you are willing and eager to accommodate to those needs, and that the quid pro quo would be her accommodation to your need for more frequent sexual relations with her. If this doesn't work, then the two of you should seek help from a marriage counselor. If that fails to remedy the situation, then, unfortunately, the basis for a divorce would be indicated. A final alternative, and one that I suggest warily as a last resort, is to discuss with your wife the possibility that, given your needs and her unwillingness to satisfy them, you seek a sexual liaison outside the marriage. Perhaps the specter of that possibility would be enough to motivate her to engage in sexual relations with you more frequently.

Ian Murray, M.S.W., Author and Senior Lecturer,
Monash University, Melbourne

∼ How is the rest of your relationship? Do you exchange affection, hugs, and smiles when you *don't* want sex? Does your wife feel she is missing something in the relationship? Sometime when you don't want sex, try to gently explore this with her. Then lead into a discussion of your sexual relationship, perhaps asking her if it currently satisfies her, after which you could tentatively express your needs, using statements beginning "I feel . . ." or something similar. Don't push or pester, and if she doesn't want to talk about it, back off—for the moment. Give her more nonsexual affection. If there is no change over a month or two, raise the issue again. If she is able to take your needs seriously, try to negotiate a compromise, such as her "allowing" affectionate sex with much less preparation, say, three times a month. Good luck!

BOTTOM LINE

⟍Although they disagree in their conclusions, both experts agree that what's important in this situation is *facing it*. Letting resentment and denial fester will lead to estrangement and possibly an affair or a divorce. The wife seems to be neurotic, and her need to have everything perfect in order to enjoy sex suggests that she may have deep-seated issues that go beyond sex. If this is the case, sex may be one casualty, but the wife's temperament is probably interfering in her life in other ways as well. The husband might ask himself how his wife's behavior affects *her* life; specifically, how her control needs get in the way of living a fuller life. Although the denial of sex is what he is concerned about, there may be many more issues that could be resolved with some counseling.

Alternatively, if it is just the denial of sex, and if the wife is intentionally using sex to keep her husband at bay, there is significant unhappiness in this marriage. The wife may not be at the mercy of a disability—instead, she may be acting deliberately. The husband's reaction should be less tolerant in this case. The bottom line is that talking, first together and then (if no progress is made) with a therapist, must be a priority. If a plan can be agreed upon to solve the problems—great! If not, perhaps this couple should consider some time apart and some independent work with a counselor.

It seems the older men get, the younger their new wives get.
—Elizabeth Taylor

> *You can only be young once, but you can be immature forever.*
> —Anon.

Age is an issue of mind over matter.
If you don't mind, it doesn't matter.
—Mark Twain

Problem 11

A FRIEND OF OURS IS ABOUT TO MARRY a woman twenty-five years his junior. Several of us have shared our feeling that this age gap is too great to sustain our continued friendship. The woman he plans to marry is adorable, and we all like her greatly. But we have grown children her age, and we find ourselves at a time in our lives when we wish to socialize with our own age-group, not our children's. Are we being selfish about this? Does our friend have a right to expect more from us?

PROFESSIONAL OPINIONS

Dennis P. Grady, Ph.D., Researcher and Assistant Professor,
Eastern Michigan University

➤ Are you being selfish? Yes. Does your friend have a right to expect more from you? Yes. You suggest that you will abandon your friend if he continues to see this woman. That puts your friend in the no-win situation of having to choose between his friends and his fiancé. He'll undoubtedly choose his fiancé and resent you for forcing him to make that decision. Our society generally frowns upon relationships that are different from the norm, and your friend will encounter a number of obstacles to maintaining his marriage. Instead of giving your friend an ultimatum, you need to give him your support. If you really consider this man a friend, and if you like this woman as you claim to do, then you should support your friend in the relational choice he makes. Encourage him, listen to him, and be there when he needs a shoulder to cry on. That's what a real friend would do.

Robert Perloff, Ph.D., Author, Editor, Researcher, and Professor, University of Pittsburgh; Past President, American Psychological Association

～I would tell the man who is getting married to remember that it is he, and not his friends, who is marrying this younger woman. Opportunities for fulfillment and happiness, like the postmaster, don't ring twice. Carpe diem—seize the moment! Tell the man to pursue a course of action that is right for him and about which he feels strongly. But before marriage he should ask himself and this woman the following questions: Does he think that she would make honest efforts to accommodate to his friends and lifestyle? Does he think that he would make honest efforts to accommodate to her friends and lifestyle? The annals of marriage are saturated with marriages of men to women substantially younger than they are. A few celebrated cases are Benjamin Spock, Averell Harriman, Lorin Maazel, and Frank Sinatra. Life is short and time is fleeting. The man should be told to listen to his own heart and heed his own mind, not those of others. Carpe diem!

Cindy Hazan, Ph.D., Author, Researcher, and Associate Professor, Cornell University

～It would be nice, for your friend's sake, if you could accept his new partner into your social group. Your preference for spending time with people more your own age is natural, but so is belching after a satisfying meal—a response most of us inhibit out of consideration for others. My point is that so-called natural reactions (which are usually selfish) can be successfully suppressed without tremendous effort. You say your discomfort is caused by the fact that your friend's intended bride is similar in age to your children, and that you'd rather socialize with people you have more in common with. Perhaps there's more to it. Situations like the one you've described often evoke feelings of guilt (Am I betraying my friendship with the former wife by welcoming the new one?) and anxiety (Will my own spouse be tempted to seek out a younger partner?). The fact is, the success of your friend's relationship will depend to some degree on the acceptance of his social network. If you banish him from the group, you'll indirectly strain his marriage. Continuing to treat him as you always have and welcoming his new wife into your circle would clearly be the friendly thing to do.

BOTTOM LINE

◆ The bottom line is that all three experts noted the same aspect of this problem; namely, it is selfish to cast the situation solely in terms of how a friend's behavior affects us! The person asking this question (a woman, by the way) is not marrying this woman—her friend is. The questioner states that she likes this woman, so this woman is undoubtedly making an effort to get along with her future husband's friends. The woman sees the importance of getting along, and the questioner would be wise to follow her example. Perhaps if she makes an honest attempt to get to know this woman, she will discover what her male friend sees in her. If she allows herself to be blinded by hidden resentments or prejudices, she will drive her friend away, because in a tug-of-war the man will surely choose his mate over his friends. If the questioner gives it an honest effort and learns, over time, that she just does not enjoy being with her male friend's spouse, she can scale down the contact or limit it to occasions at which there are large groups, so that her friend's wife is only one of many people in the room. In any case, the questioner should be polite to her friend's intended spouse at all times and treat her with the same respect she would expect if the roles were reversed.

Is sex dirty? Only if it's done right.
    —Woody Allen

> *I have learned only two things are necessary to keep*
> *one's wife happy: First, let her think she is having her*
> *own way; second, let her have it.*
>   —Antony Armstrong-Jones

Problem 12

MY WIFE AND I HAVE A BASICALLY sound marriage, but we have one major disagreement when it comes to our sex life. I believe it's appropriate for each one of us to do things the other finds pleasurable, even if the giver does not find the behavior particularly arousing. (I'm not talking about anything rough here, just stuff like oral sex and wearing sexy underwear to bed.) My wife believes that each of us should only do what he or she gets direct pleasure from—and that means that many things I would like her to do, she will not even consider. I am left feeling frustrated and unfulfilled, and my wife says I am being unreasonable. What should I do?

PROFESSIONAL OPINIONS

Gary L. Bowen, Ph.D., Author, Researcher, and Professor,
University of North Carolina

Trust, respect, empathy, and cooperation are the bedrocks of sexual intimacy in marriage. In this context, spouses are able to accommodate themselves to meet the needs and wishes of each other, even when their behavioral preferences differ. First, I would encourage you to explore the nature of your relationship with your wife from a broader perspective. Problems and issues in the bedroom rarely occur in isolation. Talk with your wife about the relationship in general and how it has evolved over time. Attempt to connect the past and present with the future—where are you heading as a couple?

Second, explore your own feelings about the sexual relationship. You describe yourself as feeling frustrated and unfulfilled. Consider your beliefs about your wife's response to your sexual overtures—emotions are based on more than experiences; they are based on your beliefs about these experiences. Be willing to confront beliefs that rest on irrational premises and that limit opportunities for relational fulfillment and growth. Third, share with your wife your thoughts and feelings about the sexual relationship and why it is important for you to try new things. Encourage her to share her thoughts and feelings. Keep your focus on the relationship. Last, be willing to seek professional help—this is a tough issue, and it will not just go away.

Carol Masheter, Ph.D., Researcher and Assistant Professor, University of Utah

➤ This couple needs to have empathetic dialogue in order to explore their expectations and feelings. Sometimes the most loving act that a couple can perform is simply exploring an impasse together, honestly and respectfully. The couple can then become closer, rather than becoming more estranged through avoidance or a power struggle. Such dialogue may be a single, short conversation or several long conversations. A short conversation might look like this:

HUSBAND: I would really like for us to have oral sex.

WIFE: I hear that you would like that, but I find oral sex degrading/scary/messy/boring. How does *not* having oral sex make you feel?

HUSBAND: I hear that for you oral sex is degrading/scary/

messy/boring, and that concerns me. I feel frustrated and unfulfilled. For me, having oral sex is the ultimate turn-on/gift of love.

WIFE: I hear that you are frustrated and unfulfilled. That makes me unhappy. What can we do so that you are more fulfilled and yet I don't feel degraded/afraid/disgusted/bored?

BOTTOM LINE

～The bottom line is that something more than sex is amiss in this couple's life. It seems as though the woman is using sex—or rather, the denial of it—to control her husband. He states that he would like his wife to wear sexy underwear to bed. Certainly, this type of expectation is reasonable within a marriage, and most people would not consider this behavior demeaning to his wife. Oral sex is also a behavior expected by many people in committed relationships. If the wife chooses not to do any one thing her husband desires, perhaps because she finds the behavior distasteful, but if she is willing to replace the behavior with something else that her husband finds erotic, the sexual problems will probably wane.

The real problem is that the woman does not place a priority on creating what her husband sees as an erotic atmosphere in their marriage. There could be many reasons for her reluctance. She could be angry about an unrelated issue and be using sex to punish her husband. Or he could be an unskilled lover who leaves her flat in bed, so she may have turned off to him. If this is the case, she should communicate with him about her sexual needs and see if he is willing to meet them. Or she could be generally dissatisfied in the marriage—or with their life in general. Any one of these types of feelings could lead to her turning off sexually.

The man should assess the situation by asking himself whether his wife seems to like sex but not to like certain specific activities he would like her to engage in. If the answer is yes, perhaps erotic videos or reading materials could get her more interested. If she is simply closed to such possibilities, the husband should try to discover the root of her rigidity. If the problems turn out to have little to do with sex, the couple could consult with a therapist to help place things in perspective and work out potential solutions. Often a couple's sex life is the first place in which more general problems emerge.

Fission after fusion.
　　—Rita Mae Brown

Love is a grave mental disease.
　　　　—Plato

Problem 13

SINCE I BROKE UP WITH MY BOYFRIEND, I have experienced intense loneliness, difficulty sleeping and eating, and anxiety in large groups of people. This has been going on for six months. Do I need to see a therapist, or is this something that will fade away on its own or in response to talking with close friends? Can friends help as much as therapists?

PROFESSIONAL OPINIONS

Kelly D. Brownell, Ph.D., Author, Editor, Researcher, and Professor,
Yale University; Past President, Division of Health Psychology,
American Psychological Association

Emotional upheaval is common when relationships end, but if the severity and duration of the distress are extreme, professional help is in order. You are experiencing some classic signs of depression and anxiety. Furthermore, you labeled the problems "intense" and they still persist after six months, so it is time to take action. Speaking with friends or tackling the problems on your own has not been sufficient, so why suffer any longer? A therapist can be objective and will have had experience with many individuals struggling with relationship issues. You will be surprised by how constructive therapy can be, even if it is brief and aimed only at this specific crisis in your life.

Jeffrey J. Haugaard, Ph.D., Clinical Psychologist, Researcher, and Associate Professor, Cornell University

➤Sometimes friends can be just as helpful as therapists. It is always good to turn to friends or family for support and guidance if you would like to. However, therapists are trained to provide the type of help that friends often cannot provide. In addition, you can talk about things with a therapist that you might not want to talk about with a friend. If talking with friends and taking their advice do not seem to be solving your problem, then maybe some discussions with a therapist would be helpful.

It sounds as if you are depressed. You have many of the emotional and physical symptoms of depression. Sometimes depression seems to get better on its own, and sometimes it does not. The question at this point is whether your symptoms are interfering with your work or your social, family, or individual life. If they are, then maybe you should try to reduce them.

Depression is a disorder that can be treated. Most research shows that medical therapy (through the use of antidepressant medication) or psychotherapy (through talking with a therapist) can reduce the symptoms of depression in many cases. At this time, it is unclear whether cognitive/behavioral psychotherapy or antidepressant medical therapy is best—and it may be that one is best in some cases and the other is best in other cases. An evaluation by a licensed psychologist or a psychiatrist might indicate whether your depression is severe enough to require medication or whether cognitive/behavioral psychotherapy would be best to start by itself.

Other forms of psychotherapy, such as psychoanalysis, Gestalt, or family therapy, do not seem to be as successful with the types of symptoms you report as does cognitive/behavioral therapy. If you decide on psychotherapy, ask your potential therapist what type of treatment he or she would give for depression. Ask about cognitive/behavioral therapy. Ask whatever questions you have and raise whatever doubts about psychotherapy you have. If you believe the potential therapist's answers are genuine and make sense, then work hard with that therapist to overcome your depression.

BOTTOM LINE

➤ The experts agree that six months of suffering is long enough. Even if friends and family tell a person not to worry, her symptoms are normal, and they will pass, the truth is that this woman is paying a heavy price in terms of day-to-day functioning. Friends and family can be wonderful sources of strength throughout life, but in some circumstances—such as this one—additional help of a more objective and clinical nature seems to be warranted. If this woman wishes to set herself straight, a limited amount of time with a therapist may make a big difference.

If the woman is determined to solve her problems on her own, she should nevertheless seek out the help and support of a group of people who meet to discuss their similar situations and problems. After six months, it seems a safe bet that she will not start feeling terrific again on her own. Plus, her extreme reaction may indicate unresolved issues that are being triggered by the breakup, and these issues may also require attention. This down period may turn out to be a good time for general emotional housecleaning, and the woman may move forward with a greater sense of peace and direction in her life as the bad feelings become understood and resolved. The bottom line is that it is time for action—definitive action. A wait-and-see strategy will *not* pay off.

*Intimacy between stepchildren and stepparents
is indeed proverbially difficult.*
    —Shikibu Murasaki

The secret of dealing successfully with a child is not to be its parent!
    —Mell Lazarus

*Beware of one who drives as if she owns the road,
especially when the car belongs to someone else.*
    —Anon.

Problem 14

I HAVE MET THE MOST WONDERFUL woman after years of thinking that I would never marry again. The problem is that she feels it is important that I support her when she disciplines my two children. I cringe when she does this, as I feel she is overstepping her role in their lives. She says that the children must learn to view her as a parent, and this includes accepting her discipline much as if she were their mother. Is there any research on this?

PROFESSIONAL OPINIONS

*Ross Vasta, Ph.D., Author, Editor, Researcher, and Professor,
State University of New York*

First of all, stop cringing. It is perfectly reasonable for your new wife to expect your children to view her as a parent—which includes some responsibility for their discipline. Second, a problem exists here only if you and she have markedly different philosophies on child rearing. If you do (and maybe even if you don't), you might take this opportunity to reevaluate your family rule structure. Research suggests that kids do best when their environments are predictable and consistent. Add to that "fair and reasonable" and you have the basis for an effective disciplinary system. Many good books are available on this topic, but sound disciplinary practices often include (a) an emphasis on the child's positive behaviors; (b) rules that are appropriate for the child's age; (c) well-defined consequences that are in proportion to the misbehavior; and (d) a gradual increase in independence and responsibility, based on the child's age and good behavior. If possible, it is usually a good idea to have the children participate in developing the system. In short, view your new wife as an ally rather than an alien, and many of your concerns will disappear.

Jay Belsky, Ph.D., Author, Editor, Researcher, and Professor, Pennsylvania State University

～However much you are attracted to and attached to this woman, you cannot lose sight of your obligations as a parent to your children. If your friend's parenting makes you cringe, you would be negligent to do nothing about it. Begin by pointing out that being a stepparent is one of the most difficult jobs in the world, and that research suggests it works most successfully when children are comfortable and trust the new parent figure. Point out further that her ultimate success will likely be dependent upon her first doing less rather than more. Make it clear that you want her to become a parent figure to your children, but that parenting works best when a couple functions as a team. This means sharing ideas and, if necessary, compromising, rather than having things all your way. Be prepared to support your friend; don't undermine her in front of the children unless their safety is clearly at issue. But make it a point to talk—repeatedly if necessary—about your concerns (and hers), out of earshot of the children. You really have two choices: short-term gain (by letting her alone) and long-term cost (to you, the children, and your relationships), or short-term cost (by dealing with the issue) and long-term gain (by strengthening and preserving your relationships).

Lewis P. Lipsitt, Ph.D., Author, Editor, Researcher, and Professor Emeritus, Brown University; Former Director of Science, American Psychological Association

～I don't think there is any definitive research on this, and in any event I would have difficulty assessing its relevance to your situation, because there are several omissions of information that might affect my advice. Recognizing that you may be a widower, I am going to assume, nonetheless, that there is "another mother" of these children in their lives. The new lady in your life may be testing you to see if you will accept her fully as both your wife and their mother. If you do not, she may not be as interested in marriage as you may be. A contest of mothers may arise if both women insist on disciplinary control of the children. This will surely stress your relationship with your lady and probably with your children as well. Candid discussion with all concerned should facilitate development of your new family.

The children must understand and agree that their new "mother" has some right to dominion over her home and thus the care of your (and her) children. She must understand that a gradual approach, with successive steps toward to "full motherhood," would be best for both her and the children; she surely does not want to generate hostile relations with them. Furthermore, you must come to accept that your new partner apparently wants to share your child-rearing tasks, and that you will have to cede some of the control, as well as the pleasures, of parenthood to her.

BOTTOM LINE

～The man in this situation is wise to realize that he is facing a serious problem. If he cringes every time his woman friend disciplines his children, he communicates to this woman that her input is unwanted. If the man and woman are building a life together, the woman has a right to have input and to insist upon reasonable behavior from the children. However, the woman should discuss the situation with the man when the children are not around—the children should never be made aware of any differences in opinion among the adults, lest they use this information to pit the adults against each other. This man should examine very carefully his expectations of his children's behavior: Has he kept his expectations low out of a desire to maintain friendly relationships with the kids? Is he competing with his ex-spouse for the children's attention, and is he thus reluctant to hold the children to a reasonable standard of behavior? This man must remember that behaviors he considers cute in his children may be seen as bratty by a newcomer.

Nevertheless, if the new woman in his life is overly harsh and/or mean-spirited with the children, this man may have to accept the fact that she is not the wonderful woman he perceives her to be. How much experience has she had with children? Do children generally like her? To assess the woman's motives—in other words, whether her behavior is reasonable or unreasonable—the man should ask himself whether, if the children behaved as the woman expects, they would be acting more maturely and would be seen by other adults as being better mannered. If the answer is yes, this new woman is pointing out deficiencies in need of repair. If the answer is no, she is being overly demanding and critical. But, as two of the three experts pointed out, a successful stepparent is one who recognizes the importance of making gradual changes in children's expectations rather than forcing a sudden shift in child-rearing standards, regardless of the superiority of the new standards. Unless this man and his woman friend act as a team and view changes as a long-term process, her need to control the relationship with her stepchildren could lead to disaster.

Of all happiness, the most charming is that of firm
and gentle friendship.
  —Seneca

> *Words can never trace out all the fibres that knit us to the old.*
>   —George Eliot

The friends thou hast, and their adoption tried,
grapple them to thy soul with hoops of steel.
  —William Shakespeare

Problem 15

MY WIFE OF THREE YEARS GOES out to dinner one night a week
with a circle of female friends she's known since college. They
sometimes stay out until 1:00 A.M., and when she comes home
(always in a terrific mood) she simply says that they talked
about "women's issues and their relationships." She plans our
entire social life around these evenings out (e.g., she never
misses her "night out with her women friends"). I, by contrast,
do not have any regular social events that take me away from
my wife, and when I am invited out I bring her along. In fact, I
consider my wife my best friend, and I cannot understand why
she doesn't feel the same way about me. I am hurt by her need
to spend so much time with her friends without including me.
When I've spoken to her about my feelings, she has simply
replied that her need for female-only companionship is normal. What should I do?

PROFESSIONAL OPINIONS

Diane F. Halpern, Ph.D., Author, Researcher, and Professor,
California State University; Past President, Divisions of General and
Teaching Psychology, American Psychological Association

◥ It's difficult to understand what your problem is without more information. Why are you jealous of your wife's desire to spend one night a week with longtime friends? You have interpreted her behavior as an indication that she doesn't feel as close to you as you do to her. You need to consider if this is an accurate description of your relationship. The fact that she enjoys an evening with friends doesn't mean that she doesn't see you as her "best" friend. Are there other reasons why you feel so uneasy about her night out? Why is it so important to you that these are "female-only" gatherings? If you spend some time thinking about these questions, you might understand what is so troubling to you, and you might find ways to deal directly with your real concern. Given that these nights are important to her and that she really enjoys them, you should tell her to have a good time. If you are feeling lonely during her "night out," you need to plan some enjoyable activity for those evenings. For example, you could volunteer to work with a worthy charity, get involved in local or national politics, develop a hobby, or just look forward to renting a good movie.

John Paul Gray, Ph.D., Clinical Psychologist, San Juan Capistrano, CA;
Past President, Orange County Psychological Association

◥ What are you worried about? Talk to her about it. Are you afraid that she'll be swept away by some strange man, or that she'll be influenced by her girlfriends? Tell her. It's an opportunity for you convey to her just how important she is to you, and to confront some of your own insecurities. Tell her how dear she is to you and how you would be lost without her. Your relationship will deepen as you learn to surrender to love. Surrender might also strengthen your self-confidence and help loosen that tight knot in your belly—you know, the fear.

Are you afraid that she will enjoy others more than she enjoys you? If this is the case, maybe you should get to work on yourself. This is the point when a lot of folks get into a therapy that emphasizes individuality and creativity. You are obviously smart enough to attract an interesting wife, so stop relying on her for your self-esteem. Start something for yourself—school, religion, hobbies, it really doesn't matter what it is, because anything *you* really enjoy will broaden you. And this will translate into enthusiasm, which not only relaxes the knot but makes you more interesting to talk to. Additionally, any activity you involve yourself in that includes other people will ultimately result in your getting feedback about yourself from them. And that feedback is fuel for growth. We are social animals by nature, and it is healthy to be engaged with others outside the primary (family) group. Good relationships are made up of two *individuals* who are each capable of functioning alone but who come together to meet husband-wife needs. The husband-wife relationship is not designed to meet all our ego needs; don't place an unfair burden on it by expecting too much. It is your good fortune to have a wife secure and strong enough to maintain long-term friends.

BOTTOM LINE

⮡ The experts converge on the bottom line that it is the man who has the problem in this relationship, not his wife. This man should get to work on himself: He should develop a close friendship or two outside of marriage, and he should take up a hobby that he will look forward to the way his wife looks forward to her evenings out. The wife is not doing anything immoral or unreasonable—she is maintaining important friendships and social contacts.

This man seems overly dependent on and restricting of

his wife. Marriages can be strengthened when both partners have interesting hobbies and good friends outside the partnership. This man has got to stop thinking about his wife as the sole source of his entertainment and social support. By placing this type of pressure on his wife, he may inadvertently push her away. No healthy person enjoys being expected to be everything in someone else's life. Luckily, the wife knows this. The husband should accept the fact that his wife can love him dearly but still need female companionship: Groups of women can talk about different sorts of things than can mixed-gender groups. Perhaps this man can discover the pleasure of same-sex friendships with groups of men!

I can't understand why more people aren't bisexuals. It would double your chances for a date on Saturday night.
—Woody Allen

Being entirely honest with oneself is a good exercise.
—Sigmund Freud

Problem 16

I HAVE A FRIEND WHO CONFIDED in me that he sometimes has homosexual feelings. The problem is that he is dating a woman he plans to marry, and he wants my advice. Is it very common for men to have homoerotic feelings and still have happy and productive marriages?

PROFESSIONAL OPINIONS

Laura S. Brown, Ph.D. Clinical Psychologist, Seattle, WA; Past President, Division of Psychology of Women, American Psychological Association

This question speaks to the notion that sexual orientation is somehow an either-or thing. It's not; most of us are sexually shades and textures rather than solid colors. The research on human sexual orientation tells us that few if any people are either straight or gay in thought, word, and deed (to borrow a phrase from the Girl Scout oath); the problem is that most people think they ought to be.

My greatest concern would be just how much your friend has homoerotic feelings. Are these occasional awarenesses of arousal by attractive and/or well-loved men, or even a few episodes of sexual contact with other men at some time in his life? Or are these obsessions that fill his mind when making love to his fiancée or that preoccupy him during masturbation? If it's the latter, your friend may want to slow down and talk to a therapist experienced in working with people's sexual orientation concerns. The gay men I know who did marry women while loving them dearly have often felt very sad for the pain dealt to their wives when they finally came out. And if your friend is preoccupied with his same-sex fantasies, he may have some self-confrontation to do.

Ritch C. Savin-Williams, Ph.D., Author, Editor, Researcher, and
Professor, Cornell University

━ If your friend told you that he has homoerotic feelings, believe him! Even though it is not uncommon for men to have same-sex attractions, because of societal homophobia very few admit to such feelings unless the attractions are fairly strong. In absolute forthrightness your friend should discuss with his partner the strength of these feelings and whether he wants or plans to act on them. A good marriage depends on the degree to which such men are honest with themselves and their partners about their same-sex attractions. With full disclosure the two can make an informed decision regarding future plans, including how best to manage his homoeroticism. Discussing the history and intensity of his attractions with a gay-positive therapist before talking with his partner may be helpful.

The most destructive route would be for your friend to act on his feelings in secrecy, thus undermining his self-esteem, damaging the principle of marital honesty and trust, and potentially bringing home sexually transmitted diseases, including HIV. With increased opportunities for developing a variety of intimate and sexual relationships, American men have available to them options other than heterosexual marriage that can lead to a productive and happy life.

BOTTOM LINE

➤ The bottom line here is clearly that this man should not be rushing into a heterosexual marriage. The first order of business for him is to slow way down, and to be honest with his partner about why he is slowing down. Otherwise, she may believe she has done something wrong, and this would cause her needless suffering. This man must do some deep soul-searching and ask himself whether heterosexual marriage is truly what he wants or whether he has contemplated it only because of societal or family pressures. If he is yielding to real or perceived pressures in making such a major life decision, he is making a huge mistake! This man must come to understand himself, his motivations, and his needs long before he undertakes a commitment that could end up making him—and his potential wife—miserable. Although it is true that people are not 0 percent or 100 percent gay, it is also true that same-sex fantasies and longings do not portend well for a heterosexual marriage.

The game women play is men.
—Adam Smith

It's the nature of women not to love when we love them,
and to love when we love them not.
—Miguel de Cervantes

Problem 17

AFTER DATING FOR TWO YEARS, I recently became engaged to a really nice guy I met at work. We are supposed to get married in eight months. Usually we are very happy together, although we certainly have ups and downs. Recently, a man I dated briefly while in college moved back into the area and called me. I was always very interested in this man, but he moved away soon after we met (he joined the service), before our relationship got serious. Now he is professing that he has thought about me for three years and has always wanted to date me more seriously. While I love my fiancé, I have felt intensely drawn to this old flame ever since his call. It seems that I cannot stop thinking about him and how attractive I find him. What should I do?

PROFESSIONAL OPINIONS

Mary A. Banski, Ph.D., Author, Researcher, and Professor,
University of Houston

While I believe it is normal to be attracted to others, even within the bounds of a committed relationship, the intensity and timing of your interest concern me. Although the engagement period is stressful, it is also a time when partners typically feel very close to each other. Second, your interest in this man seems rather strong for someone about to commit to sharing the rest of her life with another man.

Perhaps you should do some serious thinking about your satisfaction with your current relationship. Is there a fundamental part of you that is not being fulfilled in the relationship? That is, is it possible that your obsession with your former dating partner has more to do with you and your needs than it has to do with him? My advice is to cancel or postpone your wedding until you are more certain that your fiancé is the one with whom you want to spend the rest of your life. Be gentle, but be honest—you owe him that. Then search your soul to discover whether you are ready for marriage or whether you need to spend more time deciding what is important to you in a marriage.

Elizabeth F. Loftus, Ph.D., Author, Editor, Researcher, and Professor, University of Washington; President, American Psychological Society

➤ The feelings you are experiencing are natural; indeed, many people find themselves attracted to another even after they become engaged. The big question is what you do about it. As I see it, you have at least two competing responsibilities, one to your fiancé, and one to yourself—not to mention a third responsibility to the old flame. You owe your fiancé honesty, and you should give some thought to how you can disclose your feelings to him, especially if you decide to take the next step and see this old flame. You may find that your feelings are so strong that you cannot resist the opportunity to see if this rekindled relationship is real. The fact that you are engaged and having such intense feelings might mean that you are not ready for marriage, at least not until you have tested the depth of your feelings for the old flame. If the situation were reversed, and your fiancé were having intense feelings about an old flame, wouldn't you want him to get his wanderlust out of his system before committing to marriage?

One possible course of action is to have lunch with the old flame. See how you feel, but do it in a manner that is ethical and that doesn't destroy your relationship with your fiancé.

After lunch you might find that you really do appreciate what you now have. If not, and if you want to take yet another step, this will tell you something about the strength of your current commitment. One of your biggest challenges now is how to handle the situation with minimal hurt to the feelings of people you genuinely care about. Keep in mind that small hurts now may avoid big hurts later.

BOTTOM LINE

➤ Both experts agree that this woman is not ready for marriage. The bottom line is that whether she is truly attracted to this old flame because he is and always was the right guy for her, or whether she is just using the reappearance of her old flame to create an excuse to sidestep marriage because deep down she knows she's not ready, the result is the same. The key for the woman is to decide what's going on in her own mind and heart. Why did she commit to her fiancé? Did she (at the time) believe *he* was the perfect man for her? Did these feelings later abate? Or did she never feel this way, perhaps committing to her fiancé out of a need to settle down rather than out of a belief that she had found Mr. Right? Some self-examination is called for.

This old flame may prove to be as flawed as her fiancé, once she gets to know him equally well. Perhaps the real issue is a fear of commitment to anyone. In this case, the woman may wish to ask herself whether she is the type of person who always sees the grass as greener on the other side of the fence. For now, she must tell her fiancé that things must be placed on hold, but, as both experts point out, she should tell him with kindness, since apparently he has not done anything to destroy the relationship. He definitely will be hurt, and with good reason. If he, too, seems anxious to postpone the marriage, the woman will learn that her fiancé shares her doubts. And if this is the case, this fact might have contributed to the growing disaffection in the relationship.

Nothing risqué, nothing gained.
    —Alexander Woollcott

> *What's done to children, they will do to society.*
> —Karl Menninger

Children have more need of models than of critics.
    —Joseph Joubert

Problem 18

I AM A THIRTY-FOUR-YEAR OLD divorced mother of two children, a seven-year-old daughter and a six-year-old son. The public schools in our area are lousy, and for some time I have wanted to enroll my children in private school. However, money is limited, and despite our best efforts the children's father and I just can't see how we can afford two private school tuitions. While doing some part-time modeling for a department store in town, I was approached by a man who owns an exotic dance club. He asked if I would be willing to do non-nude exotic dancing, wearing a revealing bikini, in his club three nights a week in a town sixty miles away. The pay would be fantastic, and I could use the money to improve my children's standard of living and place them in private school. But I am torn because I worry about the effects my work as an exotic dancer would have on my family. What do experts think?

PROFESSIONAL OPINIONS

Gerald P. Koocher, Ph.D., Author, Researcher, and Chief of Psychology, Children's Hospital and Judge Baker Children's Center, Boston; Associate Professor, Harvard Medical School

It is important to consider your own values and beliefs, those of the children's father, and community standards. Ask yourself these questions: If I take the job, how will I feel about explaining my decision to the children, either now or as they get older? How will I feel when my neighbors, my children's teachers, or others find out about the job? (They will find out.) How will the children's father react? Will he accept this as a positive step toward better education for the children, or will he view the job as a reason to seek a change in child custody? In some communities the job would not raise an eyebrow. In other communities you would be vilified for taking it.

How your children are affected will depend on your own comfort level, their father's reaction, and the response of the community. Talk about the idea with people you respect and watch their reactions. Taking the job may benefit your family financially, but it may also have other costs. Only you can decide what is best for your circumstances, but be cautious. The sixty-mile distance seems to offer a bit of privacy. That is deceptive. Just as the club owner found you modeling at the department store, others will find you at his club. Be prepared!

Thomas O. Blank, Ph.D., Author, Researcher, and Professor, University of Connecticut

🔺 Before focusing on the effects on your family, you must ask yourself whether you think exotic dancing is immoral or degrading; some women would see it so and others not. It's not illegal or dangerous, and as described it's relatively tame in the wider world of the sexually oriented "leisure trade." But if you think it would be dirty or immoral work, avoid it. If, however, you can see it as a well-paying job you wouldn't necessarily choose if you had all options open, go for it and stay proud! It will give you the satisfaction and self-confidence of providing better for your children so they'll have more choices in life than you've had. If you respect yourself, so should the adults in your family (and ex-spouse); if they don't, that's their problem. Your children probably won't need to know details of what Mom does, but if those details do by chance come out, children are likely to be resilient with your love and support. The club being sixty miles away can provide a buffer between your family and your job, but you should not rely on that distance to "keep your dirty little secret," if you feel it would be that.

BOTTOM LINE

➤ Both experts point out that the sixty-mile distance is no guarantee of privacy, and therefore the decision to do exotic dancing must rest on other considerations. The bottom line is that, if the woman can state with pride that she works as an exotic dancer, and if she sees nothing shameful in what she is doing, she might wish to try the job. Her ex-husband should certainly be informed so there will be no rude surprises down the road.

However, if the woman feels she would have to deceive others about her vocation, she should not consider it. Sneaking around would be serving as a poor role model for her children. If she is not willing to do the work openly, she should not do the work at all.

If, on the one hand, the community is one in which religious or moral values would cause most residents and neighbors to be appalled by exotic dancing, she should avoid this type of work. If, on the other hand, the community would consider this job a big nothing, she can take it if she wishes. (There are places in the United States where being in good enough shape to be an exotic dancer would be seen as a meaningful accomplishment after delivering two children!) What is essential is that the children not be lied to and that the mother not act as though she is doing something dirty if she chooses to try the job. If she cannot maintain such an attitude, she should seek alternative employment.

A man is no match for a woman except with a poker and a hobnailed pair of boots—and not always even then.
—George Bernard Shaw

The war between the sexes is the only one in which both sides regularly sleep with the enemy.
—Quentin Crisp

Problem 19

I MET A GUY I LIKE A LOT, but when we have sex it gets rough (slapping, verbal abuse, shoving). I find it exhilarating, and we both have strict ground rules that do not involve bruising or otherwise breaking tissue. We have been experimenting with this for four months, and neither of us has wanted to escalate the rough stuff. My question is: Is this inherently unhealthy behavior, and do we need to consult a therapist if we begin thinking of marriage?

PROFESSIONAL OPINIONS

Laura S. Brown, Ph.D., Clinical Psychologist, Seattle, WA;
Past President, Division of Psychology of Women, American
Psychological Association

Consensual sex between peers is a bit like ice cream; there are lots of flavors, and one person's favorite is going to seem odd or even disgusting to another. So-called rough sex is certainly a variety of ice cream that not many people are going to pursue. The big question is really, is this truly consensual, or is one party placating the other, going along to appear sophisticated but all the while feeling uneasy? This sort of sexual exchange requires rigorous honesty from both participants and lots of freedom to say "stop" or "not now" without penalties to the relationship. Within such parameters, playing at rough sex can be appealing for some people who are pretty happy and functional. Most important is that this sexual exchange be occurring in the context of a relationship free from coercion and abuse, a relationship of equality of power and value. For example, if the names you're getting called are gender related, your play may have an unhealthy hint of the potential for violence.

Helene A. Hembrooke, Ph.D., Author, Editor, Researcher, and Postdoctoral Associate and Lecturer, Cornell University

➤ If this is the only way the two of you can get aroused, then yes, I would say there is something inherently amiss here. However, if these behaviors are indulged in some of the time as one of several approaches to sex or foreplay, then I see nothing wrong with a little roughhousing—in fact, it's probably healthy to explore these submissive and dominant aspects of yourself. Being able to engage in these kinds of behaviors requires a great deal of trust in your partner, and thus seems to reflect well on your relationship in general. Setting ground rules and experimenting indicates a willingness to communicate freely with your partner, and again this would suggest a healthy relationship. As long as neither of you feels degraded or abused, and there exists some balance between the rough-and-tumble sex and sex that is somewhat more tender and nurturing, this seems like a potentially healthy alternative to the sexual doldrums that can develop in a relationship.

BOTTOM LINE

➤ Both experts agree that rough sex can, in some situations, be acceptable. But because of their different focuses, these experts arrived at somewhat different conclusions. One problem with a relationship in which the partners engage in frequent rough sex is that often the amount of roughness necessary for arousal grows over time. At first, slight acts of roughness may create a feeling of intrigue and arousal. But soon more is needed. If this type of sexual dynamic develops, one or both partners may become injured. If the participants do indeed have strict ground rules and still find themselves getting aroused over time (despite a lack of escalation of rough behavior), there's probably not a major problem. But if sex has gotten less arousing and if there are temptations to engage in rougher and more risky behavior, it might be wise for this couple to consult a therapist.

The deeper issue in this situation concerns what does and does not create arousal for these two people. They should try to understand why they need roughness to feel sexy and attracted. There is a chance that some unhealthy needs are motivating this behavior from a deeper level. By giving in to their urge for rough sex, this couple may have made it more difficult to have enjoyable sex with others should their relationship end. The small proportion of people who enjoy engaging in such rough sexual behavior would make this couple's chances of finding new partners slight.

I deny the lawfulness of telling a lie to a sick man
for fear of alarming him; you have no business with
consequences, you are to tell the truth.
　　　—Samuel Johnson

It is always the best policy to tell the truth—unless,
of course, you are an exceptionally good liar.
　　　—Jerome K. Jerome

There's such a thing as moderation, even in telling the truth.
　　　—Vera Johnson

Problem 20

WE ARE A LARGE, CLOSE-KNIT GROUP of siblings whose father just died. The youngest sibling, my sister, lives three thousand miles away and is eight months pregnant. Our doctor told us about the many potentially negative effects of stress in the last trimester of pregnancy, including higher rates of gastrointestinal tract problems at age five among children born to women who experience intense stress in the final months of pregnancy. Here is our dilemma: Do we tell my sister that her father has just died, knowing (a) that she will be unable to attend the funeral (airlines and her pediatrician will not allow her to fly); (b) that such news could have negative effects on the fetus; and (c) that as the youngest child who was very close to her father, she may feel intense anger at having been excluded from the family's period of mourning when she later finds out that her father died and she was not told?

PROFESSIONAL OPINIONS

Gerald P. Koocher, Ph.D., Author, Researcher, and Chief of Psychology,
Children's Hospital and Judge Baker Children's Center, Boston;
Associate Professor, Harvard Medical School

━If you value the closeness of your family and respect your sister, don't exclude her at this critical time. There are lots of things that might cause emotional stress to a pregnant woman. Most of them are not under anyone's control. Wouldn't it be better to draw her into a supportive circle of family? Imagine how she would feel if she inadvertently heard the news from some source outside the family.

People cope with loss differently, and one person cannot decide the right way to mourn for another. We do know that mutual support is a positive force for coping with bereavement. We also know that participation in memorial activities is an important source of caring and renewal.

Not only should the sister be told right away but she should also be invited to become actively involved in the funeral activities. She may not be able to attend, but she can certainly be in touch with family by telephone. She can be invited to put thoughts on paper so they can be shared with mourners. The funeral or memorial service could be captured on videotape, allowing her to experience it if she wishes. In this way your sister will be told about the loss by people who share her sadness, and the closeness of the family can be strengthened despite its loss.

Alan Fogel, Ph.D., Author, Researcher, and Professor,
University of Utah

━Anger is more stressful than grief. Family secrets and paternalistic protectiveness are almost always more harmful than the truth, especially if that truth is wrapped in the bonds of love and solidarity. If the family is close-knit, then your sister can easily feel a part of the mourning process, even at a distance. The research on the effects of stress on fetal development is controversial. Effects usually come from long-term stressors, including family violence, poverty, and social upheaval, such as war. It is well documented that perceived loss of family supports and ties can lead to severe maternal depression following childbirth, which is considerably more harmful to infants than prenatal stress. Your sister should be part of the circle of family loss regarding your father's death, and everyone in the family should talk to her before and after the funeral. Plans for the next family reunion should also be discussed.

Douglas P. Peters, Ph.D., Author, Editor, Researcher, and Professor, University of North Dakota

➤ I strongly favor delaying telling your sister until after she delivers her baby. Granted, this may cause resentments in the future and undermine trust among family members. But your sister's baby has a right to be born as healthy as possible, and this takes precedence over all other considerations. None of us would condone a pregnant woman taking drugs that could have an adverse impact on this unborn child's life, and none of us ought to overlook this unborn child's right to be born free from preventable stress-related complications. (Some colleagues that I consulted with on this issue expressed the fear that if society upheld the rights of the unborn to be paramount, this could undermine abortion rights. This is not the issue, however.) Later your family can explain the reason they withheld the information about your father's death, suggesting that, had he been alive, it would have been his wish to protect the next generation of his family.

BOTTOM LINE

➤ This is a truly sad situation, and one for which there is no ideal answer. While two of the experts favor telling the sister of her father's death, the third argues against doing so on the ground that it would cause harm to the most vulnerable person, the unborn baby. The trauma of receiving the unexpected news of a parent's death right before delivering a baby is undeniably severe. However, the trauma of learning afterward that the death took place, and that numerous others knew of it but she was not told, is also heartbreaking. The grief is sure to indirectly affect the child regardless of when, precisely, the mother is told. Some research suggests that while she is pregnant the hormonal changes associated with stress may be even worse than the effect of the mother's mood change upon hearing the news after the baby is born.

One way to resolve this dilemma is to ask what type of person the sister is. Would she likely interpret not being told as an act of deliberate deception or harshness? Or would she interpret not being told as a way to shelter her, for which she would be grateful? Would she look back and say, "I'm glad I didn't know before the delivery"? Or would she be overwhelmed with resentment? If she is told of her father's death while she is still pregnant, might she become hysterical and suffer birth complications that could endanger her and the baby's safety? Clearly her doctor, as well as her husband, should be consulted before any decision is made. One way to handle the situation if the family decides not to tell is to draft a joint letter, which everyone signs and then seals and mails to one family member—so there will be a clear postmark proving when it was written. This family member can then retain the letter unopened until after the birth. In this way, the sister will know just how hard this decision was on her siblings, who love her and wish only to spare her and her child the suffering of receiving tragic news at the wrong moment.

*Older women are best because they always think they
may be doing it for the last time.*
  —Ian Fleming

A wise and understanding heart.
  —1 Kings 3:12

Problem 21

A FRIEND OF TEN YEARS has recently stated that she would like
to have an affair with me. Neither of us is in a romantic relationship at the moment. She said that no one would ever
know, and that she wouldn't place any demands on me other
than when we see each other twice a year at professional meetings. I like this woman a lot, but I am not wildly attracted to
her (or even close), so I backed off from her offer. She became
angry and said that other men would love to have this kind of
offer and that I am crazy to decline it. Physically, I would probably enjoy being with her, but would this destroy our professional relationship and our friendship?

PROFESSIONAL OPINIONS

*Lynda M. Sagrestano, Ph.D., Author, Researcher, and Professor,
University of Illinois*
➤ My advice would be not to get involved in a relationship
with this woman. First, she is a professional colleague, and affairs such as this could come back to haunt you. Second, she is
a friend, and given that you are not physically attracted to her,
if and when this affair ends, it could jeopardize an otherwise

good friendship. Third, some time in the near future one of you could become involved in a committed relationship and either have to end this affair or lie to your partner. Fourth, her anger at your refusal suggests that she may think of this as more than just a casual affair. She may believe that she will not make demands on you other than at conferences; however, it is difficult for someone to predict how she will respond in this type of situation. Finally, in the age of HIV and AIDS, casual sex and multiple partners are risks not worth taking, especially for someone you are not attracted to and with whom you don't anticipate becoming involved in a committed relationship.

Brant R. Burleson, Ph.D., Author, Editor, and Professor,
Purdue University

━Your reluctance to have an affair under these circumstances is certainly understandable. Obviously, you are under no obligation to have sex with anyone and shouldn't get involved when you don't feel good about the situation. Given the realities of sexually transmitted diseases, unplanned pregnancies, and unwanted emotional involvements, there's no such thing as casual sex. Moreover, your friend's angry reaction suggests that she has more than a casual attitude about this situation. My guess is that you'd put your relationship with her in greater jeopardy by having than by not having an affair.

Have you asked yourself why your friend wants a sexual relationship now, after ten years of platonic friendship? Maybe she just wants something physical, but sometimes people turn to sex in response to losses, relationship failures, felt inadequacies, or other disappointments. Seeking this affair may signal some personal or emotional problem she is experiencing. You can be a real friend to this woman by talking with her about her life and helping her explore her feelings. Let her know that you sincerely care about her and are genuinely concerned with what's going on in her life. Encourage her to talk at length about her feelings and really listen to what she says.

I suspect this woman needs a loving friend a lot more than she needs a casual lover.

BOTTOM LINE

➥ The bottom line is that it would be a colossal mistake to have an affair with this old friend, for many reasons, including those raised by each expert. The friendship would be ruined, the physical attraction is not even there, she does not want a committed relationship, she knows many of the man's colleagues and is involved with his professional life, and so on. Unfortunately, some men in this type of situation give in to the lure and demands of the moment and have a sexual relationship they end up sorely regretting.

The real question is why a woman would ask for such a relationship: The answer, as both experts note, seems to be that she craves more than she is saying outright. Perhaps her cravings are subconscious and she is not being deliberately misleading—or perhaps the cravings are conscious and she knows that she must be very careful about what she says. In any case, this woman needs help. She may be going through a difficult time in her life and thus be feeling especially needy. If this man truly cares for her, he will suggest that she seek professional counseling. Sex is clearly not the answer!

A man who has never made a woman angry is a failure in life.
—Christopher Morley

A marital argument can be dissected, much like a frog can,
but like the frog, it dies in the process.
—Anon.

Problem 22

MY WIFE IS VERY CONTROLLING and is also jealous of my career success. When I asked her if we could purchase equipment for a home office for me, she said we simply could not afford it. I needed the equipment, so I bought it on a secret credit card in my name and told her my company paid for it. Later she found out when she applied for a bank line of credit. She became furious and is now threatening to divorce me. I pointed out that the equipment was enabling me to get more work done and raise our family's standard of living, but she will not discuss the issue. What should I do?

PROFESSIONAL OPINIONS

Connie Schick, Ph.D., Author, Researcher, and Professor,
Bloomsburg University

Your question raises some issues about honesty in your relationship. Because you intended to buy the equipment regardless of your wife's feelings, your question was not entirely honest. Also, my guess is that your wife was at least as angry about your sneakiness in buying the equipment as she was about the purchase itself. I'm concerned about other issues as well. If your wife is in fact controlling and jealous, that is a problem. And if you are wrong in thinking that she is, that too is worrisome. You need to develop more honesty, trust, and mutual respect in your relationship, probably with the help of a marriage counselor. In the meantime, some practical steps might help. For example, it appears that you and your wife pool all your financial resources; perhaps each of you should have a certain amount of money that you can spend as you please.

Michael L. Commons, Ph.D., Researcher, Author, Lecturer, and Research Associate, Harvard Medical School

～ Several competing claims and actions are breaking your connection to each other. You secretly act on your own. Then your wife mistrusts you more and listens to you less. She does not want you to be more successful even if it helps the family, unless there is a similar investment in her future. Stand outside the arrows of blame—stop assuming that one of you must be right and the other wrong. Together, look at the interaction between you. Consider that for your relationship to work, each of you should include the other in decision making. Make clear that you understand how upset your wife is about your lying, and that you know it is wrong. You then may have a continuing dialogue with her. In your own words, repeat to her what she is saying. Then she may see that you are listening and that you care. Fit together both views on how to decide and pursue individual and family goals. Rather than having each person exercise veto power or go it alone, discuss how your wife would like to see compromises achieved. Listen to her goals for herself and the family, and share your goals. Support her pursuit of her goals. And, if either of you would like, get marriage counseling.

BOTTOM LINE

➤ Both experts point out that this relationship has major problems. The fact that a wife would flatly refuse to allow a husband to purchase equipment that would ultimately raise the family's standard of living suggests that she is a controlling and potentially mean-spirited person, more interested in punishment than in supporting her husband's goals. And the husband's behavior was also out of line. Sneaking around like a weasel and buying expensive equipment—and lying about it—is not a mature way to respond to the situation. Of course, he may have felt as though this was his only choice, and being boxed in is always difficult, but he should instead have simply stated that he needed to buy the equipment, and he should have suggested a couple of counseling sessions to discuss the purchase.

There are undoubtedly a lot more serious issues marring this relationship than the purchase of a computer, and counseling is absolutely necessary in this situation. Working with a good mediator, the husband and wife could each have a say. He could argue that the equipment purchase was, logically, something the family could not afford to bypass, since the extra income generated benefited the entire family. She could argue that she would rather have saved the money, or spent it elsewhere, giving her reasons. The money earned by the couple could then be budgeted so that purchases designed to increase their earning power would take priority (say, over purchases the wife might wish to make but which are not essential). The wife would simply have to give in on this one— or else start earning more money herself. The couple might also consider earmarking some of the money each of them earns for purchases not endorsed by the other spouse. The bottom line is that this couple has a lot more to worry about— and repair—than an expensive new home office!

Life is ever since man was born
Licking honey from a thorn.
　　—Louis Ginsberg

I would rather lie on a sofa than sweep beneath it.
　　　　　　　　　　—Shirley Conran

Problem 23

MY BOSS IS A VERY POWERFUL and influential person in our field. Since I began working for him two years ago, he has made it clear that he would like to have a sexual relationship with me. He touches me inappropriately at times, but mostly he makes sexual comments, invites me up to his room at conferences, and so on. I like my job and believe it could lead to an excellent future position at another company—but if I leave now I will have nothing to show for the past two years, and I will also have an extremely powerful enemy. If I bring sexual harassment charges against my boss, I will end up losing more than he does. What should I do?

PROFESSIONAL OPINIONS

Robert Perloff, Ph.D., Author, Editor, Researcher, and Professor, University of Pittsburgh; Past President, American Psychological Association

➤ I gather, as much from what you did not say as from what you did say, that the prospects of a sexual or romantic relationship with your boss would be unpleasant and unrewarding for you. Therefore, if I were you I would be forthright with your boss, telling him that while you respect him greatly for his professional and business skills and success, and while you would consider it a privilege to benefit from him as a business mentor and your boss, you must stop short at this point, and you are not interested in intimacy and romance with him. If this candor results in your dismissal, then so be it; the chances are that before too long you'll be able to find another equally rewarding and exciting position.

If, and this is a big if, however, you feel that under other circumstances intimacy or a romantic relationship with your boss could be pleasant and satisfying for you, providing he is unmarried, you might let nature take its course. In the course of human relationships, there have been a multitude of studies where romance and intimacy flow from what was originally a business, professional, or professor-student relationship. Perhaps, therefore, under these circumstances, you and your boss may appropriately and enjoyably extend your professional relationship into a personal domain.

Martine Powell, Ph.D., Clinical Psychologist, Author, Researcher, and Lecturer, Deakin University, Melbourne

～ The fact that you are considering leaving your job indicates to me that you are distressed about your boss's advances; so no, I do not think you should let his behavior continue. However, you may be able to resolve this problem without leaving and/or bringing charges against him. You must have a lot of skills in communicating and negotiating to have gotten where you are. You should use those skills to let your boss know that his behavior is unacceptable to you. It is very important that your response be both unambiguous and professional. Meanwhile, start documenting the dates and details of further interactions with him. If the situation continues, you may need to speak with the relevant resource person in your company and/or an attorney who specializes in corporate sexual harassment. Fortunately, there are laws set up to protect people from being exploited at work, so it may well be his career on the line here and not yours.

As a last recourse, you may have to leave your job. This may not be as big a loss as you think. You may be underestimating the marketability of your current skills and the gains you have made in your career so far. If your former boss tries to gain leverage through providing damaging references, consult that lawyer!

Bottom Line

━ The bottom line is immediately to begin documenting everything the boss does that seems inappropriate. Two years is too long to have waited to take definitive action! This woman should also consult an attorney. Even if she now has no plans to enter into any legal action, her attitude may change, and without adequate documentation she will lose this option. At the same time the woman should ensure that her behavior and performance at work are exemplary. As both experts agree, she should speak directly with her boss and let him know that she does not want this type of attention. She could consider asking for a lateral transfer in her company. Perhaps the company has someone other than her boss she can ask about this possibility. Her reason for wanting the transfer should be disguised in terms of how her professional interests might be better matched. In addition, she might consider discreetly looking for a position in another company. Much of her course of action will depend on the specifics of her situation. However, one thing is clear: She must seek outside professional help and direction to protect herself and her future rights. A boss who would behave in this way is *not* to be trusted!

Jealousy is like a hot pepper. Use it mildly, and you add spice to the relationship. Use too much of it and it can burn.
—Ayala M. Pines

Let there be spaces in your togetherness.
—Kahlil Gibran

An ideal wife is one who remains faithful to you but tries to be as if she weren't.
—Sacha Guitry

Problem 24

LAST YEAR MY WIFE MET a man at work (who is also married) with whom she has developed a very close relationship. My wife and this man have a lot in common because they both work for the same miserable boss. They eat lunch together every day, and sometimes they speak on the telephone at night about work-related matters. I know she has met his children because she has mentioned this. My wife and I have a great relationship, but her friendship with this co-worker bothers me—they just seem to be too close for comfort. I have no close female friends, and I don't see why my wife can't limit her friendships to women. What should I do?

PROFESSIONAL OPINIONS

Catherine Radecki-Bush, Ph.D., Clinical Psychologist, Researcher, and Professor, Antioch University

So this situation would not trouble you if your wife's co-worker was a woman? You seem to view friendships between a woman and a man differently than you would if these activities were taking place between your wife and another woman.

Do you believe it is possible for a man and a woman to be close friends in a nonsexual relationship?

If your answer is no, you may need to examine your underlying beliefs about friendship in general and about this friendship specifically. The work world is no longer segregated by gender, and friendships are likely to develop between people who are compatible and who share similar interests, work activities, and enemies (the miserable boss). Many opposite-sex friendships are just that and do not imply romantic involvement. In fact, work relationships that provide emotional support and encouragement have been found to be related to job satisfaction. I suggest you disclose your feelings to your wife with the goal of brainstorming a way to make yourself feel more secure about this work relationship.

Gregory White, Ph.D., Author, Researcher, and Clinical Psychologist, Redding, CA

➤ You are facing a situation many men now face in the modern work world, and some anxiety and uncertainty is certainly normal. You may also be like many men, who count on their wives for almost all their support and emotional closeness. Here are some suggestions to help you feel better about the situation. First, disclose your feelings to your wife without either blame or demands for change. You say that you have a great relationship, and sharing difficult feelings is an important part of deepening your marriage. Second, why not get to know her colleague? Perhaps a mutual family outing, or going to lunch once in a while with them, or even finding that you and he might have a friendship could help ease your mind and perhaps add to your circle of friends. Third, you may want to ask yourself if you also would like to have more or closer relationships with others (men or women). This could be a good time to find others with interests similar to yours. Finally, unless you begin to behave in ways that distress yourself or your wife, you should recognize that the situation is actually an opportunity for you both to take the time to discuss the joys and frustrations of your own marriage and to make improvements where you both desire them.

Pearl Dykstra, Ph.D., Author and Researcher, Netherlands Interdisciplinary Demographic Institute

⟋ Remember to put what is happening in the proper perspective. There simply are more men than women in the workforce. For that reason, close colleagues at work are more likely to be males than females. How many women do you meet at work? Try to understand how important it is for your wife to have a colleague who shares the difficulties she experiences with her boss. Shared misery can be quite therapeutic. Your wife appears to be quite open about her behavior; she mentioned meeting his children, and you know about their work-related phone conversations at home. She also seems to restrict the relationship to collegiality. I hear little evidence of friendly interactions spilling over into leisure time. If your wife's relationship with this man bothers you, I suggest telling her this. Try to find out what this person means to her, and express your worries. You will undoubtedly learn you have no reason to be apprehensive.

BOTTOM LINE

⟋ All the experts conclude that the solution to this problem is for the man to ask himself why he is feeling so jealous and insecure. Nothing in his wife's behavior justifies the strength of his reaction. Perhaps this man should ask himself why he is reacting so sharply. First of all, he should meet his wife's male co-worker. He should also accept the fact that it is normal for partners in a relationship to have friends of the opposite sex. As long as the wife is not trying to hide the relationship, there is very little cause for concern. Maybe the two couples could meet and share an outing or dinner. Would this co-worker be introducing the wife to his children if they were involved in some clandestine activity? Would the two of them be acting so openly in front of their own spouses? Highly unlikely, to say the least!

The husband should also do everything he can to keep his marriage happy and productive. He seems jealous because, as an outsider to the company, he cannot share with his wife the type of gossip and collaboration she gets from her co-worker. The husband should simply accept this fact—he cannot be everything to his wife. This does not mean their relationship is not wonderful and fulfilling, as he admits. He should not let his insecurities get in the way of their happiness. Having said this, the husband knows at some level that the most likely place a married woman will acquire a lover is at work. If the marriage becomes less wonderful in the future, the husband's anxiety over his wife's deepening relationship with her male co-worker may take on greater meaning. But the answer to the question would nevertheless remain the same: Discuss these feelings with your wife.

Compromise, if not the spice of life, is its solidity.
—Phyllis McGinley

Married women are kept women and they
are beginning to find it out.
—Logan Pearsall Smith

Problem 25

MY WIFE HAS JUST RETURNED TO half-time work after taking six years off to have our two children. During the last six years, money in our household has been extremely tight. For example, I had to give up my membership at the golf club, and we haven't been able to take any vacations. I have been looking forward to my wife's return to work so that our financial pressures will be eased. But she points out that she expects to be even more harried than she has been, because she intends to continue doing the bulk of child care and chores around the house in addition to her part-time job. (My career does not permit me to curtail my hours in order to help with child care and chores.) Last night my wife told me that she went to the bank and set up an account in only her name where she intends to deposit her earnings. She said she sees the money she earns as "her" money, and that she should be able to spend it on whatever she wants without discussing it with me. I cannot understand why the money I earn is "ours" but the money she earns is "hers." This seems totally unfair to me, and I am feeling very angry and resentful. What should I do?

PROFESSIONAL OPINIONS

Chris L. Heavey, Ph.D., Marital Therapist, Author, Researcher, and Assistant Professor, University of Nevada

﹂It sounds like you have an argument in your future. The key is to make it a constructive rather than a destructive argument. A constructive argument is one in which neither person says anything to permanently damage the relationship, and you both feel better after the discussion than you did before. To improve your chances of having a constructive argument, make sure you are calm when you begin. Don't start with an angry tone or an attacking statement. Second, talk about your feelings regarding your wife's plan to have her own account. There is no rule about how couples should divide their money. Simply say that you were upset when she informed you of her plan and that you don't feel it is fair to you. Third, be sure to listen to what she says. This is the hardest and most important part. Based on her forceful presentation of her decision, I would guess that she is upset about this issue, so it should be dealt with in your final solution. Remember, stay calm, listen, and keep working at it until you both feel good about the outcome. Good luck!

Stuart Greenberg, Ph.D., Author, Researcher, and Clinical Psychologist, Seattle, WA

﹂Alarm bells! Perhaps having participated in too many forensic matters, I have a hair trigger for seeing potential problems. But in this scenario I fear that it is the wife who is feeling angry and resentful, perhaps over the husband's lack of help with child care, her not really wanting to return to work, or the husband's inability to make more money. This resentment, translated into financial independence, could be a sign of her planning for serious marital disruption. Or she may just be reacting to having felt financially controlled by the previous unavoidable circumstances and want to have some fun and freedom with the new family income (and it *is* family income, not hers alone, if they live in a community property state—no matter what she says).

In either case I would propose the same course of action: The husband needs to start more discussion with the wife, and they both need to disclose the nature and the depth of their ill feelings and collaborate on solutions. On this particular issue, I see nothing wrong (per se) with each of them having some fun money. I would propose that they determine how much of their total income they can afford to spend frivolously, divide that amount between them each month, and agree that they can each spend that half without accountability. I'm crossing my fingers that the nest eggs don't become legal retainers.

BOTTOM LINE

~ This is truly a sticky wicket. It would seem that, theoretically speaking, the wife and husband should each do exactly half the work outside of *and* inside of the home. In this case, all monies should also be split exactly in half—and deposited to a joint account. But the husband admits that he does not do his share of the child rearing and housework. He may say that he cannot, but what this means is that he chose a career that would not allow him such flexibility. Did he discuss this with his wife before marriage? If she agreed that he should take a more lucrative job that would preclude his helping out at home, it is unfair of her now to renege on this agreement. If this was the case, her money could be earmarked for child care and house help to lighten her burden—rather than for golf club memberships and travel for her husband! But what if the husband works extremely hard outside the home and the wife does not? He may believe that the total amount of work each one does (combining inside and outside of the home) is equal; he may even believe that he does more. In this case, he will expect to have an equal say on how every dollar earned by the family is spent.

Perhaps this topic could be explored. The husband and wife could each describe how much work—of all types—they do. They could then try to resolve the issue of who does more, and of how extra money should be spent in order to benefit the person with the greater burden. In any case, money kept by a wife in a private account such as this is still money she has earned while in a marriage. She cannot simply squirrel it away without an open agreement with her husband.

It seems there is much more going on here than "her money" versus "our money." There are deep problems and unresolved anger and resentment, and these issues should be confronted now, before it is too late. This man may be sick and tired of the pace at work, and may be willing to pursue a different career or just slow down—and do more child care and housework—providing his wife is willing to take on greater financial responsibilities and work harder to bring in more money. If this is not an option because the wife is not capable of earning as much, she will have to face the fact that she has no right to sequester money when she does not bring in an equal share. In sum, this is a very difficult situation for both parties.

Nostalgia is not what it used to be.
    —Simone Signoret

It isn't so astonishing, the number of things that I can remember,
as the number of things I can remember that aren't so.
    —Mark Twain

Problem 26

WHY AM I UNABLE TO REMEMBER large tracts of my childhood? I have only very spotty memories of the first ten years of my life, and almost no memories from the first five years. All of my friends seem to have very vivid and detailed memories of their early childhoods. Why don't I remember my childhood, and does this signify anything worth worrying about?

PROFESSIONAL OPINIONS

Katherine Nelson, Ph.D., Author, Editor, Researcher, and Professor,
City University of New York

Your stock of early memories appears to be very normal. There are great individual differences among people regarding the age of earliest memory and the number of memories accessible from early and middle childhood. The average age of first memory is about three and a half years, but most people have very few memories before the age of five years, and many people remember little of their first ten years, as is the case with you.

A number of factors seem to relate to the accessibility of early memories. Among these are family practices, especially the degree to which parents encourage their children to talk about their past experiences and elaborate these accounts into family and personal stories. Firstborn and only children and children with greater language skills tend to have more and earlier memories from childhood. And children who have experienced moves or other changes in life patterns sometimes have fewer early memories. There may be other related factors that we have not yet identified. Thus, even if none of these factors specifically applies to you, there is no reason to be concerned. Rather, your friends seem to be unusual if they can remember many events vividly from very early childhood.

Mark L. Howe, Ph.D., Author, Editor, Researcher, and Professor, Memorial University

⬧Perhaps the most important thing to realize is that memory, far from being a stable medium like a videotape, is forever being altered, updated, and modified by new experiences. The medium in which we store our memories is inherently volatile, with its contents transformed not only by new experiences but also by how we reinterpret events in light of new knowledge. Indeed, memories from our childhoods not only come back to us with varying degrees of historical accuracy and clarity but are often more a reflection of our current needs and circumstances than anything else.

Given that it is usually unique events that survive in memory, it is often surprising that we have any childhood memories at all. That is, although many experiences seem unique at the time, they are often repeated in one form or another, are supplanted by more recent events, or are reinterpreted in light of new information and "fade" into the background of other memories. In essence, then, given what we know today about memory and its volatility, there is nothing unusual about having few early memories. Whereas some people can have memories as far back as two years of age, many individuals (including myself) have few memories until around eight years of age. Although vivid recollection of early childhood events is by no means impossible, many claims concerning graphic recall of these events turn out to be false. Despite the fact that we may feel very confident about the truth of such vivid recollections, they are reconstructions of early experiences and are often inaccurate.

The point is that your situation is not at all unusual and should not, in the absence of other memory problems, be a cause for concern. Nor is it an indication that there is something dark hidden in your past. More often than not traumatic past events are remembered quite well, particularly because such experiences are often unique and distinctive.

BOTTOM LINE

⬿ Both experts, eminent early memory researchers, point out that possessing very early memories is the exception rather than the rule. A dearth of early memories is perfectly normal and nothing to worry about. Friends who claim to have elaborate early memories may be wrong: They may have constructed what they believe are memories from stories they have been told by their families, for example. Of course, some of their memories may be factual, but still this does not mean that a person should worry about having few early memories. Despite the fact that some mental health professionals would interpret the situation as signifying that something traumatic happened during childhood (for example, sexual abuse by a trusted caregiver), having only spotty early memories does *not* mean that such horrible things happened! No therapy is called for in this case, and there is nothing here worth worrying about.

We should be careful to get out of an experience only the wisdom that is in it—and stop there; lest we be like the cat that sits down on a hot stove-lid. She will never sit down on a hot stove-lid again—and that is well; but also she will never sit down on a cold one anymore.
—Mark Twain

Don't come running to me if you get your legs shot off.
—Graffito

Problem 27

I AM A FORTY-EIGHT-YEAR-OLD WOMAN who has been divorced for six years. During this time I have had two serious relationships, each lasting approximately three years. Recently, I met a man who has totally captivated me in a way that I never imagined possible. My one worry is that he will break it off with me eventually. He has had a long series of relationships that did not go beyond a year, and I do not want to invest myself in a relationship that will end so soon. Friends who have no idea that we are involved have described to me a number of relationships he has had that sound awfully similar to ours. I have spoken to this man about my fears, and he has assured me that he is also looking for a long-term commitment, that he simply had not met the right woman before, but that now he has. Am I worrying over nothing, or is the past likely to predict the future with this captivating man?

PROFESSIONAL OPINIONS

Robyn M. Dawes, Ph.D., Author, Researcher, and Professor,
Carnegie Mellon University

⬥ Concerning this man's probable future behavior, while it is true that past behavior is not a very good predictor of future behavior, it is the best predictor we have. How the woman should view this uncertainty depends on her values for the various outcomes involved. From the description, I can infer very little about them. For example, she states that she worries that this relationship that "captivates" her will end "eventually" (one statement) or "in one year" (another). She appears to believe when she uses the term "eventually" that to be desirable the relationship must be long term, but this statement may represent little more than lip service to what she thinks she should believe. Conversely, her main concern may not be as much her *intrinsic* need for relationships to be long term as her ability as she ages to form new relationships.

Given that no matter what she decides, she is not imposing suffering on unwilling victims, I see no reason to determine her values for her. Instead, I urge her to decide what she really wants. In deciding, she should attend to her intellect *and* her gut feelings, attempting to integrate information from both rather than to subordinate one to the other. Even "cowardice" about not taking the risk of having to start over if she follows her "captivating" feelings may be a legitimate factor.

Cindy Hazan, Ph.D., Author, Researcher, and Associate Professor,
Cornell University

⬥ You're worried that this man may eventually leave you, and, if his past behavior is any indication, he may well do this. But it sounds as though you also have a history of relatively short-lived relationships. In that sense, each of you is somewhat of a gamble for the other. You also have two other important things in common—the facts that both of you are looking for a long-term commitment and both feel that this relationship is different from your previous ones. Perhaps it's true that neither of you has yet met the "right" person at the "right" time. You have to ask yourself what you stand to lose. Would you otherwise spend the next year feeling lonely? Would that be better or worse than risking another disappointment? Unless you have some reason to believe your current partner isn't being straight with you, or unless there's an obviously better opportunity that you'd be missing out on, I'd say go for it! At worst, you'll experience another loss; at best, you'll enjoy satisfying companionship for the rest of your life. As they say, nothing ventured, nothing gained.

BOTTOM LINE

～As both experts point out, one thing's for sure: A relationship with this man is far from a safe bet. Of course, it is possible that he has never before met the right woman and that this time things will be different. But it is more likely that the future will consist of a replay of the past. Sometimes, a person (e.g., any one of us!) in search of a relationship can be blinded to obvious clues that a potential partner is bad news; this is often a consequence of the physiological rush of falling in love. However, reason should be allowed to enter one's mind and influence one's behavior, even if the truth sometimes hurts.

How can this woman learn the truth about this man? One idea is that she can ask him what his past women friends have thought of him toward the end of their relationships. If he fairly describes the women's points of view as well as his own, there is some chance he has a reasonable take on his past romantic situations. However, if his view is jaded and he blames every failed relationship on the other person, this woman should move on before the dust settles. She must also accept the fact that even if he sincerely wants a permanent relation-ship, and even if he clearly sees what he did wrong in the past, he may have a basic temperament that precludes his forming a long-term, stable relationship.

Where we part company with the two experts is in our be-lief that the woman should keep seeing this man only if she is willing to take the very real risk that she will be next on his list of relationship has-beens. In addition, she must be willing to accept the fact that she may miss out on meeting a potentially better mate during the time she is investing in the current high-risk situation.

I slept and dreamed that life was beauty.
I woke—and found that life was duty.
  —Ellen Sturgis Hooper

Oh! duty is an icy shadow.
  —Augusta Evans

Problem 28

FIVE YEARS AGO, MY WIFE of sixteen years developed a progressive neurological disorder that has rendered her nearly totally disabled. The doctors say there is no hope for any improvement, and that one day in the next year or so I will have to move her to a convalescent facility. My wife can no longer speak, she can barely move, and her weight has dropped to ninety pounds: She bears no resemblance to the woman I married. I have cared for my wife at home ever since she became ill, but now I feel that I have really done everything I can. I realize that when we married I took my wife "for better or worse," but I never imagined this would mean the end of conjugal life and happiness. I believe that because I am young (thirty-eight) and healthy, it would be appropriate for me to begin dating and possibly even remarry in the future. However, I'm not sure how this decision will affect our two children (ages ten and twelve). I'm also unsure of exactly how to proceed and what to tell women I might wish to date. Can experts give me any advice? Is my desire to date appropriate? What should I tell our children?

PROFESSIONAL OPINIONS

Jacki Fitzpatrick, Ph.D., Researcher and Assistant Professor,
Texas Tech University

➤ Your desire to date is understandable. It can seem like a way to feel good again, or just make the madness in your life stop for a couple of hours. If dating doesn't seem right, think about other ways to relieve stress. Find a friend or hire a nurse while you take some time. Or find a support group—its members will understand your situation and they will offer solutions. If you date, think about how involved you want to get right now—are you looking for company or for a second wife?

Talk about dating with your kids up front—they should never find out from someone else or be surprised by your "friend." Tell your kids how you feel about your wife and dating, and how this will affect them (for example, will they get less time with you?). They may be fine with this, or they may say things that are hard to hear: you're cheating on Mom, next you'll replace them with "better kids," and so on. Reassure them about how much you love them. Their reactions will be affected by family changes, so keep an ongoing dialogue. And be honest with the women you date. This is a complicated situation, and these women have the right to know what is happening. If you wait to tell them when "the time is right," this time will never come. Your family may be too much for some women, but you'll know a lot about the character of those who stay.

Narina Nunez Nightingale, Ph.D., Author, Researcher, and Associate
Professor, University of Wyoming

➤ The situation you describe is tragic and is one that has no easy answers. My best advice is to consider two things. First, you've known and loved your wife for sixteen years. If she could speak, what would she tell you? Second, what would you want your wife to do if the roles were reversed? Would you

want her to find happiness? Let the answers to these two questions guide you.

In addition, I would say not to feel guilty about having normal feelings and a desire for companionship. You promised to care for your wife for better or worse, and as long as you make sure that she is cared for, whether by yourself or by others, you have met your obligation to your wife. If you do decide to date, you need to explain your situation to any woman you wish to become involved with. As long as your wife is alive you have an obligation to her, if only to make sure she is in a comfortable facility and is well cared for. Any woman worth your time will appreciate the fact that you keep your promises and take care of your responsibilities.

As far as your children are concerned, let them know that you still love your wife and, if you decide to place her in a convalescent facility, that they will still visit their mother. Let them know she will always be a part of the family, even when she has passed away. Explain to them that you will be seeing other people because you need a grown-up to spend time with and lean on just like they lean on you. Make sure they understand that no one will ever replace their mom. You might even tell them that you will try not to bring anyone into the family that their mother wouldn't have liked.

BOTTOM LINE

～ It is tough to be moralistic with someone facing such a grave tragedy at such an early age. For the benefit of the children, and out of common decency, this man should be honest with his kids about spending time with female friends (that's all the kids need to know unless and until a relationship turns out to be more serious). He should also be up front with any women he sees, because many might not wish to begin an involvement under such circumstances. Perhaps the best solution is for this man to seek joy through other outlets until his

wife is institutionalized to live out her remaining days. Once he has unwound a bit over a year or two, and once his children have acclimated to not having their mother in the house anymore, perhaps he could again consider beginning a romantic relationship. It may simply be too soon right now. Hobbies or clubs in which he can pursue an interest and make friends under no pressure to date would be easier ways to start living a real life, bit by bit, independently of this tragedy.

Protect me from what I want.
　　—Jenny Holzer

There is only one motivation, and that is desire. No reasons
or principles contain it or stand against it.
　　—Jane Smiley

Problem 29

I AM A FORTY-TWO-YEAR-OLD MAN, married for eight years, with one son (age five). Ever since my teenage years, I have enjoyed pornography—magazines, books, and videos. I don't like anything rough or abusive, just pictures of naked women having sex and videos of sex. I believe that my use of pornography gives both me and my wife a better sex life because it keeps me energized and interested in sex. Up until now, my wife has tolerated my use of pornography, but now that our son is getting older she wants me to remove all sexy materials from the house. She's afraid our son will stumble across my magazines or accidentally find a video. She also believes I am setting a bad example for our son by watching this sort of stuff. I don't want to stop, and I think she is worrying needlessly. What do experts think about my use of pornography?

PROFESSIONAL OPINIONS

Francis Macnab, Ph.D., Author and Executive Director and Chief of
Training in Psychotherapy, Cairnmillar Institute; Past President,
International Council of Psychologists

It is a common part of adolescent (male) development to have a fascination with sexual display. Many adults continue

that fascination as an expression of voyeurism, and as an aid to eroticism. Some partners—usually the females—are uncomfortable with such behavior and may see it as a criticism of their sexual adequacy and a threat to their relationship commitment.

I suggest the wife be helped to examine these matters in regard to her own perceived adequacy and self-esteem, her security in the marriage, and her understanding of the male's erotic exploration through voyeurism and display. The husband should be encouraged to examine whether his behavior is within the parameters of accepted normality. He would need to acknowledge that his behavior causes anxiety to his wife, and that his continued preoccupation with pornography without adequate discussion and acceptance by his wife could be disruptive to his marriage.

Both parents might recognize that young people have strong sexual interests and urges, and their fascination with pornographic literature should be fully recognized and discussed. In doing this, the son may be encouraged to develop a more open respect for the human body and what an informed and enjoyable sexuality can mean.

J. P. Watson, M.D., Author and Professor, Guys Hospital, London
～ It is worth asking what the word *pornography* may mean here. For a man who "enjoys" it, the idea (if spelled out) is likely to be something like, These visual images increase my sexual arousal, at least in part by encouraging me to imagine that I am doing enjoyable sexual things with the person(s) portrayed in the material. However there is no escaping the fact that the "material" portrays real people who are almost certainly being exploited. In addition, obtaining sexual arousal by these means is likely to divert attention from the development of a closer marital relationship. Your wife's attitude regarding the possibility of your son's discovery of your activities is an extension of these concerns, since she is worried that your son might develop a compromised image of his main male role

model, which might impair his personal development. Hence giving up pornography should allow marital and family relationship enhancement.

BOTTOM LINE

━These experts analyzed the problem differently, focusing on different factors. So it's not surprising that they arrived at different conclusions. Obviously, this is a tough situation because the wife tolerated the husband's use of pornography until recently. Now that the son is getting old enough to discover the father's pornographic materials—or even to surprise Daddy in the act of watching or reading these materials—the wife has become anxious. Had the wife felt strongly enough about this subject, she might not have been willing to marry this man unless he abandoned the use of these materials. But she went ahead with it, and the man has been using the stuff all his adult life—apparently without incident or problem— yet now he is being required suddenly to give it up.

If the wife's true and sole concern is her son discovering the materials or his father while using them, the situation can be dealt with by having the father keep all materials locked securely at all times, and having the father use the materials only behind a securely locked door, while the boy is asleep. But it is possible that the wife's concerns are more far-reaching. Sometimes a person can look past a partner's faults and live with the situation until children come along, but then ideas regarding what constitutes appropriate behavior and a sound role model become stronger. A person may suddenly see a partner's behavior as potentially damaging to a child, and new demands may then be placed upon that partner, who may balk. Perhaps the wife can attempt to come to terms with what exactly is bothering her about her husband's use of pornography. If she absolutely cannot tolerate the behavior anymore, the husband will have to face the dilemma of losing the pornography or losing his family.

Of all the animals on earth, none is so brutish as man
when he seeks the delirium of coition.
  —Edward Dahlberg

The most exciting attractions are between
two opposites that never meet.
—Andy Warhol

Problem 30

I MET THIS WOMAN I REALLY LIKE. We share similar tastes in foods, films, and values. I really enjoy being with her. The problem is that I do not find her as sexually exciting as other women I have known whom I have not liked as much as her. Objectively speaking, this woman is attractive, so that is not the problem. We have talked about this and tried to do things to put spice into our lovemaking, but nothing seems to last. I know that she would like to get married, and part of me would like to as well. But I am worried we could be making a mistake if we got married and then our sex got even less exciting. What do experts say?

PROFESSIONAL OPINIONS

Laura S. Brown, Ph.D., Clinical Psychologist, Seattle, WA;
Past President, Division of Psychology of Women, American
Psychological Association

➤ In the best tradition of answering a question with a question, I would wonder, how central is sexual excitement to your overall sense of personal and relationship satisfaction? I wonder this because the reality is that many things can happen in a

long-term relationship that interfere with, diminish, or even
wipe out sexual contact between partners without seriously
damaging the sense of passion, connection, and commitment
in those instances when sex qua sex is not the most central
thing. And in relationships that are very sexually exciting,
there may be less sense of companionship, respect, and care.

So I'd suggest that you assess yourself honestly. If sexual
excitement is extremely important to you, you may be taking a
risk by making a commitment to this woman. If, alternatively,
you find that it's important, but not as important to your sense
of satisfaction as are other elements in the relationship that are
clearly present, you may want to rethink your beliefs about the
necessary components of a happy long-term relationship. Sex
has been a little overrated as the end-all-and-be-all of good relating, and certainly very bad sex, or extreme imbalances between the desires and appetites of partners, can be harmful to
a relationship. But you're not talking about bad sex here, just
ordinary, day-to-day sex, the kind that most people seem to
have as their relationships mature, deepen, and go on.

David F. Ross, Ph.D., Author, Editor, Researcher, and Assistant
Professor, University of Tennessee

➤ Sex is really important (particularly if a person isn't getting any), so the thought of this man being married to a woman
with whom he shares a lackluster sex life is terrifying. I believe that he should not marry her unless the lackluster sex life
can become dynamic and exciting over time. What has this
couple tried? Whipped cream, strawberries . . . how about sex
on the beach in Tahiti? Great sex isn't just luck: It takes work,
imagination, and creativity. If sex is a fizzle already, this relationship is in trouble. I say he should not marry her but should
try to work on building a great sex life, or else agree that both
can seek sexual excitement outside the marriage and leave it
at that. Of course, another (more cynical) opinion is that after
marriage, there is not much sex anyway, so if this man is convinced that marriage is for him, this woman is the perfect

choice: He likes her now and the sex isn't great, he probably won't find the sex much improved after marriage, and so there will be no surprises and no disappointments!

BOTTOM LINE

⌐The man states that he likes this woman, enjoys being with her, and shares her tastes and values. He has even contemplated marriage with her. But she is not the most sexually exciting woman he has ever met. Well, perhaps he has to grow up a bit. If other women excited him because they were "bad girls" or were mysterious in some way or unattainable, these characteristics may have accounted for their sexual attractiveness. If so, this is a situation in which a dose of maturity—which would include accepting that sex isn't the most important thing in life—may help the man move forward. Perhaps his ambivalence about committing is responsible for keeping the relationship from becoming more sexually satisfying. If so, resolving his ambivalence might lead to better sex.

If, however, the man feels that there is something central missing in his "brother-sister" type of relationship, he should cut the woman loose and go back on the market. In this event, it could be that the label "ordinary sex" is being used to disguise his beliefs that other important relationship elements are lacking as well. If there is simply no chemistry, marriage is not worth pursuing. But if this is the case, he should make the decision now and move on. To stick around without intentions of developing a deep love and commitment would be unfair to this woman, who deserves someone who both desires and is committed to her.

All marriages are beautiful. It's the living together afterward that's difficult.
—Abigail Van Buren

Do not mistake a child for his symptom.
—Erik Erikson

If a child lives with approval, she learns to live with herself.
—Dorothy Law Nolte

Problem 31

MY HUSBAND ALLOWS HIS SEVEN-YEAR-OLD daughter from his previous marriage to sleep in our bed whenever she has a bad dream. Lately, this has turned out to be every night that she stays at our house. I believe this is a bad precedent—she is old enough to sleep in her own bed, and I believe that he should comfort her, then insist she return to her room. My husband says I am being unreasonable and that her behavior is normal and will pass. What do experts think?

PROFESSIONAL OPINIONS

Barry Fallon, Ph.D., Author, Researcher, and Senior Lecturer, University of Melbourne; Past President, Australian Psychological Society

It is just inappropriate for a seven-year-old daughter to be sharing the marital bed on a regular basis. It is not normal and will not simply pass. You have two problems to address—one concerns your husband and the other your stepdaughter. If the daughter is really having bad dreams whenever she stays in your house, you need to establish what is causing this to occur. If she is using "bad dreams" as an excuse to get into bed with you and her father, this needs to be dealt with and stopped. The stopping of it has to come from her father. Discuss with him why he is so ready to accept her in the marital bed. Are there other things not right with the relationship between you and him? Is he being used by his daughter to assuage his guilt for not being with her on more occasions? There is no reason why he should not be able to give her the reassurance that is necessary while she is in her own bed.

Douglas P. Peters, Ph.D., Author, Editor, Researcher, and Professor,
University of North Dakota

～You should be more tolerant of your husband's dilemma: He has divorced the mother of his child and now has the task of retaining his daughter's love and affection, despite potential attempts by his ex-wife to alienate him from his daughter (this often happens, especially since he is remarried). Before you pass judgment on the appropriateness of the daughter's behavior, you should know that in some cultures across the world it is considered completely normal for children to share their parents' bed. The daughter's behavior is probably the result of insecurity and feelings of being excluded by her father's new relationship. Perhaps she actually is having bad dreams—divorce can be extremely unsettling and stressful to a young child. After all, her parents admitted they did not love one another anymore, and she may see herself as being responsible for some of the dissent between them. She may also see herself as being next on her father's list to be rejected.

You made the decision to marry a divorced man with a child. Now his problem is your problem, and you must help him solve the problem and make his daughter feel more secure and nonthreatened. Do you do everything you can to show attention to the child when she is with you? Do you talk to her, play with her, and so on? Try to approach the problem from the perspective of making the daughter more secure, and you will undoubtedly find that over a couple of months she will no longer wish to share your bed. For example, begin by allowing her to stay in your bed long enough to calm down, then returning her to her own bedroom.

Mary Lyn Huffman, Ph.D., Author and Visiting Assistant Professor, University of Sewanee

━ I agree with the stepmother. The child should be comforted and returned to her room. The problem as I see it is related to one of two issues: (1) The child could in some way feel uncomfortable with the stepmother and, therefore, may seek comfort from her father and reassurance that she is still an important part of her father's life. This comes in the form of competition with the stepmother. Thus, by sleeping with her father, she is able to be closer to him and in a sense come between the two of them. (2) It might also be that the child is unsettled by her father's divorce and recent remarriage. I would be interested to know what sleeping behaviors are encouraged or tolerated at the biological mother's home. The best situation is for the father to discuss clearly these different issues with his daughter and determine what can be done during waking hours to strengthen both his relationship with his daughter and her relationship with his new wife. Her seeking comfort by sleeping with her father might be an indirect way of communicating that she feels distant from those she needs to be attached to. Incidentally, in no way do I feel that this sleep pattern signifies a previously abusive relationship between the father and daughter.

BOTTOM LINE

━ The experts don't see eye to eye on this one. We think this man must recognize that his new wife is bound to feel extremely uncomfortable with his seven-year-old daughter sharing their bed. It is the man's responsibility to deal with this problem, both quickly and effectively. First, he should ask himself about the broader context of the child's life and the impact her parents' divorce has had upon her: Is the child generally happy and secure? Is she doing well in school? Does she have friends? Is she otherwise normal? Also, the man should examine the quality of the child's relationship with his new wife: Do they get along well? Is the new wife kind to the child? Is the child angry about his remarriage? Is the child possibly using the bad dreams excuse to separate her father from his new wife? Is the child jealous? In addition, the man should ask himself about how his current relationship with his ex-wife may be affecting his daughter.

Perhaps a father-daughter heart-to-heart talk could help smooth things out and get to the focus of the child's worries. This father could take pains to spend a certain amount of quality time alone with his child to ensure she does not feel excluded from his life. At the same time, he must insist that she sleep in her own bed. If she complains of nightmares, he might take her back to her own bed and sit with her for a short time to reassure her. But he should not allow her to sleep in his bed for any reason. If these efforts are not successful and if the child becomes despondent or depressed, the man should seek professional help for the child. She may be going through a tougher time than he realizes.

There are a number of mechanical devices which increase
sexual arousal, particularly in women. Chief among them is the
Mercedes-Benz 380 SL convertible.
    —P. J. O'Rourke

            Money is not an aphrodisiac: The desire it may kindle
            in a female eye is more for the cash than the carrier.
                        —Marya Mannes

To dream of the person you would like to be
is to waste the person you are.
    —Anon.

Problem 32

I AM A THIRTY-SIX-YEAR-OLD UNMARRIED man with a powerful and prestigious career and a substantial amount of money. I would like to marry and have a family, but I am worried about women wanting me for my position and money instead of for who I am. My male friends say not to worry—they say that I earned my money and that this *is* who I am. But I would prefer to find a woman who cares for me because of who I am *inside*, not someone who would grow dissatisfied with me if my fortunes turned. What should I do?

PROFESSIONAL OPINIONS

Pepper Schwartz, Ph.D., Author, Researcher, and Professor,
University of Washington
➤ This is an astute question to ask, because no matter what anyone says, money does matter: It is part of what attracts many a woman to a man, and it may, even unconsciously, loom larger than almost any other attribute you possess. Of course, people never say they marry for money—but have you ever

noticed how few women fall in love with men below their own families' income level?

So what's a guy to do? First, marry a talented, ambitious, financially successful woman who doesn't really need to bask in your success or seek salvation under your star. You'll know your money isn't everything to her because she can provide for herself. But in case this isn't possible or desirable to you, make sure you date someone a very long time; check out her character and how materialistic she is. Test the relationship well. Not everyone is dazzled by money and prestige. Still, keep in mind this thought: Money can corrupt a relationship and change it from a love affair to a business relationship. Best protection: If you don't marry someone who wants to be a princess, you won't have to worry about maintaining a castle.

Marshall Prisbell, Ph.D., Author, Researcher, and Professor,
University of Nebraska

━ First, I would try dating a couple of women at a time and avoid discussing your financial status. Try to select women with various career backgrounds. They may have the "money" concern as well. After a month or so of dating a particular woman, I would openly discuss my relationship concerns. Continue dating this person until there is trust and a sense that the relationship is not based on the reward of money. Talk about what you like about each other. If you enjoy various activities together, share mutual friends, and there is talk about a future, then you probably have a satisfying relationship and need not be concerned about whether the person likes your money over you.

Keep in mind that relationships do not grow overnight. It is important to take your time in selecting a compatible mate. Eventually, if there is liking and possible love, you will grow together, having mutual respect and trust. You will have experienced many events together, such as the first fight, the first sexual encounter, the first favor or gift, the first vacation together, and so on. If both of you enjoy each other's company, stay together. Most important, keep talking. Your conversations will tell you if there is trust in the relationship.

My final suggestion would be to relax when you are dating. Do not think that your dating partner is after your money. You must have confidence that you have other positive relationship qualities. Be secure with yourself and present this image early on while waiting a bit to mention your concerns. Good luck and much relationship success.

Helen Cowie, Ph.D., Author, Researcher, and Professor,
Roehampton Institute, London

⌐ The outer trappings and power do not seem to have given you any deep sense of self-worth, belief in yourself, or even understanding of who you are. I suggest that you first get in touch with your own inner self. How can you do this? I recommend that, with the help of a counselor or psychotherapist, you start the long but rewarding process of exploring your own inner world and learning how to take the risk of sharing it. In the beginning you will find that you become ready to relate in an open and genuine way to the people around you. My hope would be that by relating in this new way, you discover those who share your concerns, so you may be able to identify those people, men and women, who can offer real friendship. Out of these experiences may grow love. As Shakespeare wrote:

Love is not love
Which alters when it alteration finds
Or bends with the remover to remove.

Thomas Joiner, Ph.D., Author and Research Clinical Psychologist,
University of Texas

⌐ You weren't always powerful and rich. When you were in your twenties, to which of your qualities did women respond? How did you know they were responsive? Answers to these questions may help you distinguish nowadays between women who are interested in you and those who are interested more in money, power, and prestige. You mentioned your male friends, who said not to worry. What about female friends? Seek their advice. Your question involves assessing someone's underlying motivations—often not an easy task! On the one hand, if money, status, and so on do not motivate a potential partner in other areas of her life, it is a good bet that they won't motivate her choice of a mate. On the other hand, someone being interested in money, status, and so on does not necessarily mean that she is only interested in your money. It will come down to how you feel with the person—if you feel consistently attended to and appreciated over the course of a fairly long dating relationship, chances are that the person is interested in you, regardless of her interest in money or status.

One other note: Evolutionary psychologists believe that evolutionary pressures have selected for different mate-selection strategies for men and women. According to this view, men select mates on the basis of health, reproductive potential, and the like, whereas women select mates based on status, access to resources, ability to provide, and so on. While this is a controversial view, there is good scientific evidence to support it. The upshot of this view for you may be reassuring. Women may be attracted to your capabilities (i.e., potential to provide and gain resources)—stable traits—and not so much to your current status and resources, which may fluctuate somewhat.

BOTTOM LINE

〜 The first thing for this man to do is to understand himself and his own motivations. It sounds as though he is convinced that most women will be interested only in his fortune. Perhaps he has come to view himself as a cash cow. Perhaps his self-perspective is dominated by his career and related accomplishments. This man could benefit from taking up a hobby or pursuing an activity that has nothing to do with his career and in which his fortune will not be obvious to anyone. Through this activity he could gain a sense of self-worth by being competent at something that does not involve money. Learning a sport or outdoor activity that does not require much money might be a good start. He should focus on competence instead of competition—his work life is probably filled with competition as it is, so his recreation life should not always be.

With regard to meeting women, this man should use two approaches. First, he should try meeting women through his outside interests, such as hobbies or outdoor activities. These women will have absolutely no idea about his fortune, and he should keep it that way. Perhaps he could date a woman he meets in this way, only revealing the truth about his money far down the road, after he is assured of her affection. He should refrain from choosing expensive restaurants and the like, and focus on more moderately priced spots to go on dates. A second approach he might try would be to date only well-off women he meets through work—professional women at his own level, with a lot of money of their own. These women will not be interested in becoming financially dependent on him, and he might be able to create a relationship with such a woman on the basis of love instead of financial need.

Last of all, this man should realize that not all women pursue men for money. He may view women in generally negative terms, and if his view is jaded, some counseling might be in order. If he has a negative view of women, any relationship would be doomed regardless of whether the woman knew about his money, since he would interpret her behavior as being money-oriented even if it was not.

The child is father of the man.
—William Wordsworth

He that spareth his rod, hateth his son.
—Proverbs 13:24

It is a wise father that knows his own child.
—William Shakespeare

Problem 33

I AM ENGAGED TO THE MAN of my dreams: He is warm, caring, honest, and an all-around great guy, with one big exception. His ten-year-old son from his previous marriage is a beast, and he just doesn't see it. Everyone else who has met the boy sees it, though—he has been in constant difficulty at school, he has been in trouble with the police for starting fires, he is rude and offensive to my fiancé and me, and when criticized he becomes violent and impossible to control. My fiancé admits his son is "difficult" but attributes his bad behavior to "a phase." I wonder whether it is wise to proceed with my marriage plans. My fiancé and I have discussed having a child of our own, but I am in doubt about his fitness as a parent. Except for this area, though, he is a great person, and his son would only stay overnight with us two weekends a month. What should I do?

PROFESSIONAL OPINIONS

Nelly A. Vanzetti, Ph.D., Clinical Psychologist and Author, Tulsa, OK
➤ My congratulations on not being so "blinded by love" that you failed to see this enormous problem with your fiancé. You are absolutely right to be worried about this—especially since the two of you might choose to have a child of your own. Your

description of your fiancé's behavior reveals a significant problem of some sort. It may simply be a lack of parenting skills or it may be some more difficult problem, but either way, the time to iron this out is before the wedding. Have a serious, calm talk with your fiancé in which you let him know that you are very concerned about the situation. Ask him to go to counseling with you (and perhaps also his son and ex-wife!) so that you can get to the bottom of this, even if it means postponing the wedding. If he refuses, he is clearly not the man of your dreams!

Campbell Leaper, Ph.D., Author, Editor, Researcher, and Associate Professor, University of California
～ Your fiancé's denial regarding his son's conduct disorder is a very serious matter. Starting fires, violent behavior, and school failure rarely are only "a phase" in a child's life—especially if they are not directly addressed. Therefore, if you marry this man, his son's problems are apt to become a regular presence in your life. I also wonder if the way your fiancé relates to his son tells you something fundamental about how he approaches relationships over time. What does his downplaying of his son's behavior problems tell you about this man's ability to deal with problems in a relationship? Will he similarly ignore difficulties and problems when they arise in your relationship or with a child that you might have together? Ignoring his son's conduct disorder suggests that this man is not quite as "honest" and "caring" as you imagine. You need to confront the grave nature of the situation with your fiancé now. Ideally, your fiancé and his son will enter into family therapy. Otherwise, "the man of your dreams" may turn out to be the harbinger of your worst nightmare.

Martine Powell, Ph.D., Clinical Psychologist, Author, Researcher, and Lecturer, Deakin University, Melbourne
～ You are very wise to address these issues now, before you decide to go ahead with the wedding. Given your description

of your fiancé, the relationship holds a lot of promise; you say he is a caring, honest, and tolerant man. But when you marry a father, you acquire a son. It sounds like this boy has serious problems that are unlikely to go away without assistance. I believe that you, your fiancé, and the boy would benefit from seeing a specialist who has expertise in child behavior problems and parent management training. The biological mother would also need to be involved in some way, regardless of whether the child exhibits these behaviors when he stays with her. All this is daunting, but there are effective ways of helping families in such situations, provided that you and the boy's other caregivers are willing to work together.

It is important to remember, though, that the boy's behavior is only a problem for you if you decide to marry this man. While you are weighing the cost of this problem against the benefits of continuing the relationship, it may be helpful to consider the following issues. First, the boy will be a dependent for several years. Do you harbor feelings of anger and resentment about having to take on this "extra baggage"? Second, are you *and* your fiancé willing to take on the responsibility needed to initiate change? Third, you have presented your fiancé as all good (except for his parenting) and his son as all bad, which may not be helping you to think clearly in this difficult situation. What has your fiancé done to contribute to his son's negative behaviors?

BOTTOM LINE

━ Here's a case in which the three experts not only see the problem the same way but arrive at similar conclusions as well. This woman must ask herself what type of man would look past such unacceptable and dangerous behaviors on the part of a child. Most mental health professionals would not view fire starting, violent behavior, and ongoing disruptiveness in a child as simply a "phase." No matter how wonderful this man may seem as a potential life partner, there has to be more to this story than meets the eye, in particular, problems with the man's character and values. The first order of business is for this woman to postpone her wedding plans indefinitely. The word *danger* is written all over this situation. Second, as the experts advised, she should insist that the man and his ex-wife seek professional help—and that his son be required to attend regular counseling sessions—in the hope that this dysfunctional family may get back on track.

It is possible that in the distant future the situation may improve significantly, making marriage an option once again. Unfortunately, however, given the severity of the boy's behavior, it is far more likely that things will not improve measurably, and in this case this woman should not contemplate marriage to this man. There may be deep pathology in the man, his ex-wife, or both, and there certainly is deep pathology in the son. This is not a situation worth wasting one's life on as an outsider. The smart money says to get the heck out, now, and recommend the professional assistance this family so badly needs. This father may have a responsibility to stick by his son—but this woman does not!

You can only be young once, but you can be immature forever.
—Anon.

You're never too old to become younger.
—Mae West

They say a man is as old as the women he feels.
—Groucho Marx

Problem 34

I AM A FORTY-FOUR-YEAR-OLD SCIENTIST, and I just met an attractive twenty-four-year-old graduate student at a university where I gave a talk. We hit it off right away at the dinner in my honor and afterward began corresponding over E-mail. Both of us are mindful of our large age gap and differing career trajectories, so we agreed to go slow for a while and just be friends until we decide if a deeper relationship is feasible. My problem is that several friends of mine have been openly critical of me, making jokes about my "midlife crisis" and suggesting that I get a tattoo and motorcycle to complement my "trophy." Most of my friends have been polite to the woman's face, but two have been openly rude. Are they seeing something I missed, or can we make this work despite our differences in age and career trajectory? What should I do?

PROFESSIONAL OPINIONS

Narina Nunez Nightingale, Ph.D., Author, Researcher, and Associate Professor, University of Wyoming
➤ Maybe you should think carefully about why you're attractive to this twenty-four-year-old student. Your friends are

probably teasing you because you may be playing out one of the oldest clichés—that of an older man trying to regain his youth. Maybe that's not what's happening in your case, but you have to realize that's what your friends think.

Before taking this relationship any further, analyze your motives. Before meeting this student, did you go through a divorce? Were you beginning to feel old? Were you feeling inadequate? If you answer yes to any of these questions, you may have fallen into this relationship to help bolster your ego and to make yourself feel young and attractive again. If that is your true motivation, this relationship was doomed from the beginning. A young lady, no matter how engaging, cannot give you back your youth or help you feel better about yourself. Only you can do that. My advice in this case would be to end the relationship.

However, if you carefully analyze your motives and realize that you are sincerely attracted to this young lady and she to you, and you realize that you share a deep bond, my advice would be to tell your friends to go to hell and pursue this relationship. No relationship comes with guarantees. Granted, you may have some additional hurdles to jump, but you can't win if you don't play the game. As the hockey superstar Wayne Gretzky so aptly put it: "You miss all of the shots you don't take."

Douglas P. Peters, Ph.D., Author, Editor, Researcher, and Professor, University of North Dakota

➤ Relationships are never easy to maintain, especially in today's climate of self-centered casualness, or what I like to call the Jerry Seinfeld syndrome. Persons with this syndrome believe that each of us is at the center of her or his constantly changing universe, and that any one mate is substitutable for any other depending on how that person makes us feel at that particular moment. In my opinion, it is not enough that you and this twenty-four-year-old have a powerful attraction to each other, for this will surely ebb over time. And she is not likely to remain at the center of your universe, nor you at hers, unless there is a solid core of shared values and aspirations. Such shared values are unlikely to be present in a relationship that spans different generations. In the bright, hot blush of romantic and sexual attraction, you are likely to be blinded to this reality, but trust me that it is there! In a couple years, each of you will be tempted to focus on these generational differences to justify arguments and advocate for changes in the relationship. Relationships are hard enough without adding this kind of burden.

My advice is, start asking yourself what it is about this young woman that draws you to her. Is it her tight skin and naïveté? Is it her innocence and willingness to look to you as the leader in the relationship? If you stop to analyze the situation, it should be clear that if any one these factors is driving your attraction to her, the relationship is doomed. If none of these factors is behind your attraction, there is absolutely no reason to be involved with a person her age. Either way, the relationship is fighting an uphill battle. I think you ought to begin looking for women closer to your own age. At least the inevitable struggles can be met on equal terms.

Martine Powell, Ph.D., Clinical Psychologist, Author, Researcher, and Lecturer, Deakin University, Melbourne

⬤ I am not entirely sure what the problem is here. Is it knowing how to respond to your jealous friends? Or is the problem the age difference and the viability of the relationship? Either way, you should have more faith in your ability to make decisions. You already have a hypothesis—that this is a potentially important relationship—and you are currently testing it. As you follow that through and allow the friendship to develop, you will know if a deeper commitment is feasible. Any relationship you choose to enter will have potential difficulties to negotiate, and there is never a guarantee of success.

As for your friends, they will probably adjust to the idea of this relationship in time. Meanwhile, why don't you spend some time meeting this woman's friends? If you are going to go further with this relationship, they will also be a part of your life.

As a caveat, I am assuming that you are not in an adviser-advisee relationship with this woman and that her academic career does not depend on decisions you will make. The power dynamics in this type of situation are unbalanced, and the probability that one of you will get hurt is high.

Ann P. Ruvolo, Ph.D., Author, Researcher, and Assistant Professor, University of Notre Dame

～ I won't say to stop dating her, because things could *possibly* work out. However, many things are against you, so it's wise to go slowly. Differences in experience and resources make it hard for you to be equal partners. The status difference between an established scientist and a student also causes a power difference. In addition, when your partner graduates, if her interests and goals change, you may grow apart.

Only you can know your true feelings and whether your attraction is caused by a midlife crisis. I don't think it is, because if it were, you would not be moving slowly and trying to be friends first. In an insensitive way, your friends raised some issues. If it is helpful to consider these issues, do so and form your own judgment. If they are wrong, don't be concerned about their comments.

Additionally, true friends would not ridicule either of you, much less be openly rude. They would act out of concern for you. You need friends who are more supportive and respectful. Take time to decide what truly is best for both of you. If you both address these concerns, you may have a satisfying relationship.

BOTTOM LINE

ᴥ Here we have four experts who agree on some points and disagree on others, with the result that they come to very different conclusions. We think the bottom line is that, for this man, caution is clearly in order—both in dealing with his new woman *and* in dealing with his friends. Working at building a friendship with the woman is the first order of business: If this relationship has any potential, there must be a solid foundation for the future. The second order of business is reconciling what the friends are saying—which, incidentally, is probably a lot worse when they are gossiping privately. The man may not care what his friends say, but they may well have a point. However, there is no excuse for their rudeness, particularly in front of the woman herself.

Any time a relationship is marked by substantial age and power differentials, as is the case in this matchup, there is clearly another latent agenda motivating the parties. This man would be wise to maintain his friendship, and no more, with this woman while he allows his libido to subside and perhaps stops thinking with his "southern brain." At the same time, he should insist upon reasonable treatment by his friends, or dump those who claim they are his friends but who insist upon embarrassing him and acting openly rude to someone he cares for.

Going to work for a large company is like getting on a train.
Are you going sixty miles an hour or is the train going sixty miles
an hour and you're just sitting still?
—J. Paul Getty

The trouble with the rat race is that even
if you win, you're still a rat.
—Lily Tomlin

The only thing achieved in life by standing still is unemployment.
—Anon.

Problem 35

EVERY TWO YEARS FOR THE PAST eight years my husband has been transferred by his company, and we have moved our family. This has become an exhausting series of moves, and every time we settle somewhere, we have to pack and leave! I don't think this is good for our children, who have never had much stability in their lives. Plus, it is tough for me to find a job wherever his company sends him. He is well paid and enjoys his job, but I have become very resentful and have even thought of asking for a divorce, despite the fact that our relationship is otherwise strong. When I bring the subject up, my husband just says, "What can I do? I have no choice and good jobs are hard to get." Am I being unreasonable?

PROFESSIONAL OPINIONS

Jill M. Hooley, Ph.D., Cognitive Therapist, Author, Researcher, and Professor, Harvard University

➤You and your husband need to talk at some length about this issue. Whether anyone is being unreasonable or not depends very much on the circumstances your husband is facing at work. What are the consequences to him if he does not move? If he leaves his present job, what are his prospects for getting another comparable position locally? Moving so frequently is clearly disruptive for everyone. But your husband losing his job would also create problems. If this is a very real possibility, and he genuinely has no choice in the matter, you have only two choices for yourself. The first is to divorce your husband. This makes no sense if your relationship is otherwise strong and if you truly value stability for your children. The second is to go along with things and make the best of the situation.

Rather than resenting what is happening, is there a way that you can begin to view these circumstances as providing opportunities for you and your children? What are your own goals? How important is your job to you? Do you need to keep struggling to find a job in each new town, or do financial circumstances permit you some other options, such as taking classes or developing other interests that you may have? The more you (and your husband) can think about this problem in a flexible way, the less trapped you will feel by the situation.

Karen H. Bonnell, Ph.D., Researcher and Associate Professor,
University of Southern Indiana

━No, your feelings aren't unreasonable, but I hear you telling me the stress of constant change associated with your husband's employment has reached a "critical stage." Change can be good, especially when we see it as progress toward a satisfactory goal; but I hear you describing it as being dragged from one place to another, uprooting the children, and creating instability in all your lives. It's possible your husband shares your feelings but is afraid of resisting job transfers because doing so might jeopardize his employment. Rather than facing this fear, he chooses to avoid it by accepting the transfer assignments.

It is important that you share your feelings with your husband. He may guess that you aren't happy with the situation, but it is imperative that he knows you feel the situation has become a "job versus family" crisis. By sharing your feelings with your husband, you should also encourage him to share his feelings with you. You might discover that your husband sees the transfers as opportunities to move up within the organization, and that his perception of moving every two years is not the stressful family ordeal you perceive.

You should also look objectively at your children's behaviors to discover if moving has indeed been detrimental to their development. Do they make new friends, are they performing well in school, and do they have good relationships with each other and with you? If you discover/uncover a pattern of negative behaviors in your children that might be related to the relocations, then by informing your husband of your discovery you may help him come to realize the severity of his moves' impact on his family. You also might discover that your children are not greatly affected by the relocations and that your resentment is based primarily on how you feel.

The first step in resolving this crisis is to identify it as such and to begin openly sharing your feelings with your husband. The next step is to objectively assess how the situation has affected the family relationships and the children's development. Finally, you and your husband must concur that the situation should be addressed together, that both of you must agree on the best solution for the family, and that it must be a solution you can support without resentment and hostility. It took years to build up to this family crisis, but with some patience and open communication, both of you should be able to resolve it.

BOTTOM LINE

⌐ First, this woman must ask herself whether the situation was one she knew about before she married this man. If the answer is yes, and if she made a deal that included being willing to move regularly in exchange for her husband's good job, high pay, and security, then she really must do her best to live with the situation. If, however, this woman did not make a commitment based on her husband's current job requirements, she has a right to state that she feels worn down by these demands. Her children do need stability, and she herself has a right to put down roots and live in one community for more than two years.

As both experts pointed out, this woman and her husband should ask themselves about their options. If she expresses her deep feelings of resentment to him, he may agree to change jobs, if this is possible. But doing so may mean a loss of money, and lifestyle changes, perhaps dramatic ones, may be required. Or he may be a middle-aged man who has no other career options. In this case, what exactly does she wish him to do? How much money can she earn, and how does she expect the family to survive? If the children and the parents would all suffer greatly from a lack of income, be forced to live a meager existence, and so on, would these trade-offs be worth it to her? Has she ever asked herself this question? This woman must identify the real options.

If the husband has other options but has been unwilling to pursue them because he likes his job and does not want to give up promotions or make less money, perhaps the wife should tell him he must make a choice between his career in the fast lane and his marriage. If he truly has an option that would be somewhat less palatable to him, but that would allow the family to stay put, he has a responsibility for the good of his children and his wife to accept it.

The only unnatural sex act is that which you cannot perform.
—Alfred Kinsey

The best book for two people to read to improve their love life is
the chronicle of each other's feelings about themselves.
—David Vescott, M.D.

Problem 36

MY HUSBAND OFTEN WANTS ME TO perform various sexual acts that I find either demeaning or insulting to women (oral sex, vibrators, wearing sleazy evening apparel). I told him that sex can never be good if one party feels "used," which these acts make me feel. My husband points out that when we were dating I was willing to do these things, and he doesn't understand why it is a problem now. It is true that I used to do them, but I felt pressured and didn't have the guts to tell him. He seems to regard marriage as a license for each partner to expect the other to pleasure him or her, even when doing so does not result in sexual arousal for the other partner. What do experts recommend?

PROFESSIONAL OPINIONS

J. P. Watson, M.D., Author and Professor, Guys Hospital, London

One might suppose that mutual respect is an admirable feature of a continuing, committed relationship. This must involve each partner doing or not doing things only and precisely because the partner himself or herself desires it. This "policy" contrasts with a model of marriage in which the husband decides what happens and the wife is required to accede to the husband's wishes. This usually implies a double standard, for example, excusing infidelity in the male but not in the female. If the husband is uncomprehending of what appears to be his wife's change of inclination, he should ask himself whether she may have moved on from an earlier subservient approach to a need for a more mutual and equal relationship approach. I would advise the husband to spend more time trying to identify and meet his wife's needs, and less time trying to satisfy himself at her expense.

Carlfred B. Broderick, Ph.D., Author, Researcher, and Professor, University of Southern California; Past President, National Council on Family Relations

～I regret that we live in a society that considers it reasonable for a woman to have to seek "expert" validation for establishing boundaries on the uses of her own body. Beyond that, it saddens me to be reminded of the extent to which many view sex as some sort of Olympian gymnastic sport in which one's partner is cast in the role of apparatus. What a waste of sexual potential! Without attempting to oversimplify or over-romanticize the matter, if one of the chief functions of sex in a marital relationship is not the reinforcement of trust and unity and uniqueness, the loss to the couple is incalculable. By definition, such a relationship cannot be imposed. It is reciprocal, mutually respectful, joyous, and emergent. It unites the body and the soul of each partner and of the couple. If this couple is getting less than this, they are being cheated.

BOTTOM LINE

～Both experts' conclusions flow logically from their analyses, but we disagree with these experts' analyses of the woman's plight. We think the husband has a right to be confused! While he was dating his future wife, she engaged in the sexual activities he enjoys, and she appeared to enjoy them. Then they married—so of course he assumes she enjoys sex with him. This is a reasonable assumption on his part. He may have chosen to marry this woman precisely because she seemed to enjoy the same sexual activities that he enjoyed. Now, all of a sudden, she turns the tables on him. Now the activities are disallowed, and she feels demeaned and insulted. This is not fair—she should have made her views about these sexual activities clear to her husband the first time he asked her to participate in them. Instead, she went along. Now he finds himself married to a woman who does not wish to do what he enjoys. He told her ahead of time—what more could he have done?

Still, if the woman loathes the activities, we agree with the experts that she should not be expected to perform them out of a sense of obligation. The bottom line is that the woman's failure to communicate created this situation. Now she must take responsibility for creating a solution. She should be honest and tell her husband that she lacked the courage to speak openly in the past. Furthermore, she should consider counseling, reading erotic materials, or exposing herself to alternative sources of erotic information in an attempt to loosen her attitudes. These sexual acts are shared by many couples who find them pleasurable. They are not inherently degrading; this judgment is being made by this woman for her own reasons. What makes a given act degrading is often simply the attitude of the person performing it. Perhaps the wife can examine the basis for her negative attitudes and change them. She owes her husband an honest attempt to more closely approximate how she behaved before marriage. (If the husband is doing more to make her feel degraded than she admits here, counseling is definitely in order.) This is not to say she should do things she loathes, but perhaps there are activities her husband would like that she would not find reprehensible and might even learn to enjoy.

My little old dog, a heart-beat at my feet.
  —Edith Wharton

*I am simply delighted that you have a Springer spaniel. That is
the perfect final touch to our friendship. Do you know there is always
a barrier between me and any man who does not like dogs?*
  —Ellen Glasgow

*I loathe people who keep dogs. They are cowards who
haven't got the guts to bite people themselves.*
  —August Strindberg

Problem 37

I AM ENGAGED TO A WONDERFUL MAN, but last night he told
me that he wants me to find new homes for my two dogs before he and I move in together. I was shocked! These dogs
have been my family for seven years, and I love them very
much. My fiancé isn't allergic or anything, he just says dogs are
too much trouble and he doesn't want to deal with the inconvenience. He has never had an animal and has never seemed
particularly fond of the dogs. He told me he knows at least one
couple who would be willing to give the dogs a good home
where I could visit them regularly. What should I do?

PROFESSIONAL OPINIONS

Frank E. Millar, Ph.D., Author, Researcher, and Professor,
University of Wyoming

This sounds like the first of many "power struggles"
about your "family." Which other relatives will he find "too
much trouble"—your parents, siblings, friends? Take a stand
now before a pattern develops in which your fiancé does not
want to "deal with the inconvenience" of your family. Yes,

marriage is a long-term commitment requiring mutual accommodations, but this claim about your dogs sounds like the first move in a pattern in which your family will be discarded or, at a minimum, not shared and not enjoyed together. Relatives, friends, and activities need not be enjoyed equally. However, the right to engage in these relationships and actions must be respected. However honest your fiancé may feel in stating his preferences, your right to express your preferences is being degraded and denied. Your family is part of you, important to you, and it comes with you. To discard them is to negate the you that both you and he know. If you are not allowed to share your "family" with your fiancé, do you want to be his spouse? I wouldn't.

Michael E. Roloff, Ph.D., Author, Researcher, and Professor, Northwestern University

ᴥ Given that you want to keep your relationship and your dogs, you must find a creative way to solve this problem. Although it is unacceptable, your fiancé proposed a solution that would allow you to visit your dogs. In response, you must create a plan whereby the dogs remain with you but do not become an irritant to him. First, you must have your fiancé explain the specific reasons he does not want the dogs to live with you. "Trouble" and "inconvenience" are too vague. Ask about his particular concerns, and propose specific solutions for each one. I suspect that he will raise legitimate problems you have already solved. Second, do not demand that he "learn to live with the dogs." Clearly, you are the one who wants them, and the burden of dealing with future "dog hassles" will probably fall to you. Finally, do not sit around and mull about the problem. That will only make matters worse. Confront the situation calmly and honestly. If you passively give up the dogs, you could become resentful. If you force your fiancé to accept them, they could become the topic of ongoing argument. Find a solution that meets both of your needs.

BOTTOM LINE

⬿ The one thing this woman should clearly *not* do is give up her dogs and proceed with the marriage. This would be a course of action she would deeply regret. First off, she must remember that the dogs are not new on the scene—they were a part of the package deal that she offered to her fiancé, and that he accepted. Where was the talk about not liking dogs when they were first dating? Perhaps if her fiancé had made his attitudes about pets clear to her back then, as a pet lover she would have concluded that they had no future together.

Often people who like animals and people who do not find that they have many other differences as well. This man sounds as though he was waiting until there was a commitment to spring upon his fiancé the need to dump the dogs. He was using a "foot in the door" method to break it to her slowly. But these dogs are her family, and they were important to her long before she met him. If he is willing, she could consider a compromise in which the dogs are banned from certain parts of the house, and in which she takes care of the dogs. Unfortunately, though, it sounds as if the man is not thinking along these lines. If she proposes such a compromise and he rebuffs her, she should accept that he is not the man she should be spending the rest of her life with! First, he wants to dump the dogs; next, he will want to change a million other things about her. If he won't accept a compromise, she should accept the fact that he is not Mr. Right and put him out to pasture. At least she won't be lonely at night in bed.

Comfort easily merges into license.
—Miriam Beard

Is it not strange that desire should
so many years outlive performance?
—William Shakespeare

It's never too late to have a fling,
For Autumn is just as nice as spring
and it's never too late to fall in love.
—Sandy Wilson

Problem 38

I AM A DIVORCED, CHILDLESS WOMAN in my midfifties, currently involved with a very sweet and decent man in his early sixties. I have been single for over ten years and have always assumed I would remain single—one divorce was enough for me! But my current man has suggested that we marry so that each of us has "someone to grow old with." Although this man is my best friend, and I love him dearly, I am not "in love" with him—there's just no electricity. I like my life alone, and I have become somewhat set in my ways. He says we can continue to maintain separate homes for now, but that if we marry we will have a secure emotional and financial commitment to one another as we both grow older. What should I do?

PROFESSIONAL OPINIONS

M. Broese van Groenou, Ph.D., Author, Researcher, and Centre
Coordinator, Vrije University, Amsterdam

Right now it is too soon for you to get married to your male friend. Even at an older age, one needs some "electricity" to get married. Sure, your friend is right in that you might need each other in the future, but it is very likely that he will need you more than you will need him. Because you have no children of your own, you may be afraid to grow old with no one to take care of you. Yet, since you are several years younger, you will probably end up taking care of him during the last years of his life, while you are still in good condition. If you love him, you will carry this burden of caretaking. But if you have married him only for reasons of security, you might end up disliking him and the situation he brought you into. At this moment you still enjoy living on your own, so I'd suggest you follow your heart and ignore the rational arguments to share a household. At some time in the future, you may develop a need for commitment, and that will be soon enough to get married.

Victoria Hilkevitch Bedford, Ph.D., Editor, Researcher, and Assistant Professor, University of Indianapolis

~You do not sound interested in marriage. If only passionate love would make it worth giving up your life as a single woman, then this is not the man for you to marry. Knowing this, you were wise to reconcile yourself to a single life. Few men are available at your age, and passionate love is no basis for a stable marriage (research indicates it lasts six months to two years). The only arguments you've given in favor of marriage are his reasons. Unless you share his desire for commitment, if you marry him you may grow to resent the burdens inherent in a shared life. For instance, marriage to an older man often involves a period of caregiving; given that you lack a shared history, what will help to sustain you through this arduous task? In short, it seems unwise for you to give up your current state of contentment to live with another person when you express no desire to do so. The safe choice for you is to remain single.

Douglas L. Kelley, Ph.D., Researcher and Assistant Professor,
Arizona State University

ᴥ I think that overcoming your feelings about the divorce and your comfortableness with living alone are really peripheral issues. The critical issue is whether you love this man enough, and in the right way, to warrant marrying him. You mention that you love him but are not "in love" with him. You say that he is your "best friend"; is your love for him different than for other close friends you have? If so, you may be experiencing "feeling in love" differently now than in past relationships. Also, while I don't recommend marrying just to "keep him," you must ask yourself if you are willing to risk losing this man by saying no to marriage. Often when a partner desires a change in the relationship, such as getting married, if his or her goal is blocked he or she will create change by lessening the relationship involvement. Your partner is right—marriage can encourage the longevity of a relationship. However, marriage usually comes with a whole new set of expectations that should be of concern. Examine your love for him. Then do what is best for you, the relationship, and, in the long run, your man.

BOTTOM LINE

ᴥ We agree with the three experts in advising this woman to put the brakes on getting married to this man. As people grow older, their needs from a relationship or a marriage may be different than when they were young. The man sees himself growing older and wants the security of a committed bond. However, the woman enjoys her independence and likes things as they are. Perhaps she should ask herself how her financial condition looks projected well into the future. Would marriage create greater security for her, or is she financially set as she is? Are there other reasons for getting married? In general, this woman's reluctance clearly suggests that she should wait. But she says she loves the man dearly, and presumably does not want to lose him. Thus, a heart-to-heart talk is in order. She should ask this man how desperate he is for marriage and why, what he sees as the pros and cons, and how he will respond if she says no—or no for now, at least. Is he willing to wait? Or will he leave her and seek someone else who does wish to marry? With this information in hand, the woman can ensure that her decision is made with eyes open. The bottom line is that she should not marry him, at least not now, unless there are pressing reasons to do so.

Children can't be a center of life and a reason for being. They can be a thousand things that are delightful, interesting, satisfying, but they can't be a wellspring to live from. Or they shouldn't be.
—Doris Lessing

Nothing has a stronger influence psychologically . . . on their children, than the unlived lives of the parents.
—Carl Jung

Problem 39

MY WIFE SEEMS TO BE OVERLY ATTACHED to our two children, ages four and five years. I have suggested that we take a week-long vacation alone together this summer, in which we can re-discover the relationship we had before our lives became filled with the responsibilities of child rearing. My wife's mother and my mother are both willing to watch the children. But my wife just keeps repeating that the children are too young, and that she doesn't want to leave them alone. In fact, she has never gone anywhere overnight without them since they were born. I feel that it is time for us to teach our children that they can get along without us, and time for us to be alone for a week or so to work on our own relationship. What do experts think?

PROFESSIONAL OPINIONS

Frank Fincham, Ph.D., Author, Researcher, and Professor, University of Cardiff, Wales

➤ You are right. Couples with children do need time alone to sustain and nurture their relationships. But how much couple time is needed and how it is created will vary from couple to couple. Even spouses within a couple may differ in the amount of time they feel is needed and in their views of how to create time together. Like most things in marriage, these matters need to be discussed. Important considerations include your children's age, their previous experience of being away from their parents, and their relationships with their grandparents. Right now a weeklong vacation would not be in your children's best interests or your own—can you imagine your wife being relaxed and enjoying the time together? Why not do things gradually? Let the children spend afternoons and then full days with their grandmothers. Help them to develop good relationships. Then have a grandmother do the evening routine with them in their own home. When this is going well, go on a date, and call them just before bedtime. Your children and your wife need support building up to an overnighter. Providing such support is more likely to lead to quality time together.

Sanford Braver, Ph.D., Author, Researcher, and Professor,
Arizona State University

⟍I feel it is definitely a good idea for you and your wife to take a vacation together without the children. Many husbands feel neglected after children come into a marriage, and you have been rather stoic to delay reattaching to your wife for so long. The foundation of the family is the parents' marriage, and the children's well-being will certainly be enhanced in the long run by activities that strengthen it. Some caveats: First, a week seems to be outside your wife's "comfort zone"; can you compromise on, say, two four-day trips? Second, I assume your children know their grandmothers well. If so, the visit will be healthy for the children even in the short run, but if not this may be a problem—again solvable by a shorter stay away. Finally, your wife's reluctance to leave the children even overnight for five years is unusual, and may reveal problems within her or, more likely, in your marriage. Some frank talk about what her concerns say about your relationship, preferably with the aid of a marriage specialist, would definitely be in order.

BOTTOM LINE

━ These two experts are really on the ball. It's tough to add anything to their answers. The bottom line is that this woman has got a problem, and the situation has been allowed to fester for five years. Children need to be left in the care of other relatives and responsible adults starting when they are young and flexible, or else they can develop unhealthful levels of attachment to their parents. Similarly, parents need to have time away from their children. This is especially true of married couples, who need time to be together as couples without the kids along.

Despite all of this, however, the wife sounds like she is too nervous to enjoy a whole week without her children. In addition, the way to deal with a situation in which everyone agrees that one party is being unreasonable is not to hammer this person over the head and force her—that would be a recipe for disaster. Thus, an incremental approach will be necessary. The children must become acclimated to spending time with their grandmothers and then should stay overnight at their grandmothers' while the parents are in town. Once the children are happy with the grandparents, the wife will feel better. Next, this couple should try a single overnight trip, followed by a three-day weekend, and work up gradually to a week away. This strategy may allow the wife to unwind and enjoy herself more readily.

Finally, if the wife remains unwilling to budge, even knowing that her children have responsible caretakers, she should seek professional help to explore her anxiety and unhealthful attachment to her children. She should attempt to understand what is really bothering her about being away from her kids, because her attitude is not in the children's (or her own or her husband's) best interest.

Things forbidden have a secret charm.
　　—Tacitus

The only way to get rid of a temptation is to yield to it.
Resist it, and your soul grows sick with longing
for the things it has forbidden to itself.
　　—Oscar Wilde

Many a woman in love with a cleft chin makes
the mistake of marrying the whole guy.
　　—Graffito

Problem 40

I AM A THIRTY-EIGHT-YEAR-OLD mother of three children, aged six, eight, and eleven years. For the past three years, I have been wondering whether my husband of fifteen years might be gay. There were always certain things about my husband that I didn't quite understand, such as his extraclose relationship with an unmarried male childhood friend with whom he spends a lot of time alone, and the way he would always notice other men's appearance. But our marriage is a happy one, and we have always been very good friends and very supportive of one another. Plus, he is a terrific father. I've spoken to him about my worries, but he has insisted they are groundless—though his answers always seem evasive and he asked me to drop the subject. These days I find myself wondering more and more about his feelings for his male friends. What should I do?

PROFESSIONAL OPINIONS

Kenneth M. Cohen, Ph.D., Author and Staff Psychotherapist,
Cornell University
　It is unclear whether your growing suspicion about your husband's "extraclose" relationship with a childhood friend is

the product more of jealousy—that he notices and spends time with someone else—than of concern that he may be gay. It is certainly possible for heterosexual males to develop close, nonsexual relationships with each other. Even if he is erotically attracted to males, your husband may have no desire to act on these attractions. In either case, further communication is necessary. His apparent unwillingness to engage you at length on this topic suggests that couples therapy may be indicated to help both of you clarify the nature of your relationship; the extent of your husband's homoerotic desires and whether he wishes to act on them; whether you want to remain married if he is attracted to males; whether you need to initiate safer-sex practices; and, perhaps, your feelings of inadequacy and rejection when he admires or spends time with others. If your husband refuses to explore your concerns, you must decide whether you can live with the ambiguity concerning his sexuality. Regardless of his sexual orientation or the nature of your relationship, it is vitally important to keep him intimately involved in the children's lives.

Helene A. Hembrooke, Ph.D., Author, Editor, Researcher, and
Postdoctoral Associate and Lecturer, Cornell University

⌁ That your husband notices what other men are wearing and has a close male friend hardly makes him a shoo-in candidate for being gay. I would bet that you have at least one very close female friend, and have on more than one occasion commented (probably negatively) on what another woman was wearing at some social gathering. My point is simply this: that one close friend and attention to appearance do not a homosexual make! If these are your only indicators, and if your husband (and his friend) has denied the allegation, I'm not sure there is anything else for you to do. But I would strongly suggest that you give some thought to why this is such an issue for you; I suspect it would have little to do with your husband's sexuality. If, however, there is more to your suspicions than you have revealed here, such as a declining interest in sex with you, periods of unaccountability, emotional withdrawing, and so on, counseling might be worth pursuing. Obviously it would be optimal if your husband would agree to attend, but if he refuses, go for yourself anyway. Behaviors such as these do indicate a problem, and you'll need help to prepare yourself and your children for the answers to your questions.

BOTTOM LINE

➤ Both experts remarked that the wife obviously has an issue with trusting her husband. Why? She is suspicious, and she seems to suspect the worst. Perhaps what appears to be evasiveness is simply her husband's embarrassment in answering his wife's questions. If he is not gay, being questioned about his relationships with other men may make him quite uncomfortable. But women do not often suspect their husbands of being gay without evidence (in fact, most women would not admit to seeing the evidence even if it was staring them in the face!), and sometimes this evidence may consist of subjective impressions rather than objective truths. It might be helpful for this woman to speak to a therapist on her own, in order to understand better her worries.

If her husband is indeed gay, he may be extremely reluctant to admit it, especially given that he is the father of three young children. If her suspicions appear to have a bit of truth this woman might consider letting her husband know that she understands homosexuality is not a conscious choice but rather a genetically influenced biological disposition. Thus, she could state that if he is gay, she knows he did not do this deliberately to hurt her. She might also consider speaking confidentially to her husband's close male friend: Does he seem to be gay? Does this man have any women in his life? More information would be helpful. If the wife fails to confront her worries, they may erode the marriage (and especially the couple's sex life). So it would be best for her not to ignore her feelings and impressions but rather to talk about them and get to the bottom of why she feels suspicious.

What loneliness is more lonely than distrust?
    —George Eliot

> *Man's most valuable trait is
> a judicious sense of what not to believe.*
>   —Euripides

Happiness is the perpetual possession of being well deceived.
    —Lytton Strachey

Problem 41

MY GIRLFRIEND OF ONE YEAR HAS just told me she is pregnant and would like to get married, but I suspect that the child may not be mine. The reason for my suspicion is that she continued to be close to her ex-boyfriend during our relationship, speaking to him frequently on the phone and seeing him from time to time—although she insisted they were only friends. I was careful to use condoms whenever we had sex, and it doesn't seem possible to me that I impregnated her. I have considered asking her to submit to genetic testing to determine whether I am the father, but I am afraid that this will be a very bad way to begin a long-term relationship if it turns out I *am* the father! I worry that my suspicions may be unfounded, and I do not want to hurt her in the event that the child is mine and we end up marrying. What should I do?

PROFESSIONAL OPINIONS

Perri B. Druen, Ph.D., Researcher and Assistant Professor, York College
➤Without genetic testing, no man is guaranteed of his paternity and can only trust his partner. You, for whatever reason, are suspicious (note that condoms are not fail-safe). Under the circumstances, you would best serve everyone's interests by asking for reassurance, and possibly genetic tests. Consider

the long-term consequences of remaining silent. At minimum, you're not being honest about your feelings. You may continue to feel you must censor yourself, and your partner may be burdened by guilt—either of which could erode the relationship as much as or more than discussing the issue. Even worse, the truth could be revealed under negative circumstances, such as during a custody battle or if the child faced serious illness and needed to know the biological father's medical history. Then, you and the child may suffer horrible feelings of betrayal. Furthermore, the biological father would have long been denied his parental rights. Be aware, however, that your partner may not be certain which of you is the father and may feel very vulnerable. Be supportive, not accusatory, while asking to be convinced of your paternity. You could try framing it in terms of your own insecurities. Also, think through your intentions before asking.

David F. Ross, Ph.D., Author, Editor, Researcher, and Assistant Professor, University of Tennessee

～ This man should ask his girlfriend to have the genetic testing. In view of the fact that she has continued seeing a former lover, allegedly for platonic reasons, I think that a little caution and self-protection are warranted. If the woman can't understand his caution given this background, he is obviously with the wrong woman. Given his suspicion, I would hope that he would have the strength and integrity to confront her directly or get out of the relationship. That is, if he is compelled even to *think* that she may cheat on him, he shouldn't be with her. The fact that he is suspicious means that something is wrong—regardless of whether his suspicion is correct or incorrect. Personally, I don't even like pondering the idea that I would be with someone who I'd suspect is cheating on me! Ick.

Ann Levinger, Ed.D., Clinical Psychologist, Amherst, MA

～ As I see it you have at least three serious questions: (1) Is your girlfriend pregnant by you or by someone else? (2) How can you find out without hurting her and damaging your relationship? And (3) should you and your girlfriend get married? It is clear from your writing that you understand how complex your situation is. On the one hand, you have serious doubts about whether or not this is your child and need some proof that it is. On the other hand, you realize that if your girlfriend has in fact had intercourse only with you, your insistence on genetic testing will be offensive to her. You are probably aware that even though you were careful to use condoms whenever you had sex, it is possible that you did impregnate her. A fact sheet available through Planned Parenthood states that among couples using condoms perfectly, there is a 3 percent failure rate in the first year of usage. Therefore you cannot be certain that this is not your child.

In your letter you imply that if the child is yours you will "end up marrying." You did not say how old you and your girlfriend are or how much family support you have. If your girlfriend were not pregnant, would you two want to get married? Is getting married the best or only alternative open to you? If the child is yours, you do have legal responsibilities for child support and moral responsibilities for being a father. Ideally these responsibilities will be met naturally within a close and loving family, but a marriage filled with hurt, disappointment, suspicion, and anger is not in anyone's best interest. Are you willing to do what it takes to create a good marriage?

Your first step is to listen to your girlfriend—her hopes, worries, fears—and then to tell her yours. Perhaps even show her the concerns you have written out here. It will be hard to tell her your suspicions without having her feel threatened; however, if you do have doubts about her faithfulness and about your paternity of her child, you will need to struggle through this with her. If the two of you find it too difficult to discuss your situation clearly on your own, you should find someone else you both trust to help you think and talk things through. This could be a professional counselor, or a trusted family member or friend.

BOTTOM LINE

➤ Two of the three experts agree that the man must ask the woman to undergo genetic testing to establish the child's paternity, and that he should postpone any decision about marriage until he has done so. Given the depth of his worry and insecurity, this is the only option. The woman will likely respond negatively to his requests, and he should prepare himself for this fact. Consider the situation from her point of view: On the one hand, if she was absolutely faithful to this man and if he is definitely the father, she will be horrified at being unjustly accused of straying. On the other hand, if she did have sexual relations with her ex-boyfriend (or with someone else), she will be terrified of having this behavior exposed. Of course, it is always possible that the man in this scenario is the father despite the fact that the woman was straying—so genetic testing cannot completely cure the man's suspicions about her behavior! But at least this man can make a decision regarding potential marriage that is based on a true knowledge of his paternity. Otherwise, he would be left with unresolved issues that would threaten his attachment with the child and ultimately cause more harm than good to both the child and its mother.

As two experts note, another point for this man to consider is whether he and this woman should contemplate marriage at all, given the nature of his feelings toward her and his trust in her—or lack thereof. Perhaps he could meet his financial obligations and have appropriate custody of the child a portion of the time without entering into a marriage in which he would be fundamentally uncomfortable. Since the man never mentions having a strong and deep love for this woman, he should not rush into a marriage. Rather, he should wait to see if a greater bond develops between them as a result of the birth of the child.

Anybody who goes to see a psychiatrist
ought to have his head examined.
  —Samuel Goldwyn

Psychiatry is the care of the id by the odd.
  —Anon.

Problem 42

MY FRIEND WENT TO SEE A THERAPIST several months ago for some problem that made her unhappy in her relationships. Now she is even more unhappy. My question is: Can going to a therapist make you worse off than if you never went? Are the techniques that therapists use validated in scientific studies?

PROFESSIONAL OPINIONS

Sol Garfield, Ph.D., Author, Editor, Researcher, and Professor Emeritus, Washington University

It is difficult to give you an adequate answer without knowing more about the therapy your friend received. For example, how many sessions did she attend, and whose decision was it to end the therapy? However, speaking generally, in perhaps 5 percent to 8 percent of therapy cases, the patient may end up worse than before, and the reasons could vary from case to case. Clearly, the type of patient, the kind of therapist, and how these two interact will influence the outcome of therapy. Consequently, although considerable scientific research on psychotherapy indicates that a majority of patients tend to improve, one must always remember that the individual factors mentioned determine both the process and the outcome of therapy. Some very disturbed individuals, those who are not interested in therapy, or others who relate poorly to people, may secure poor results. In a similar way, inadequately trained, insensitive, and overly authoritarian therapists may secure poor results, particularly with patients who themselves have difficulty with therapy.

Hans H. Strupp, Ph.D., Author, Editor, Researcher, and Professor Emeritus, Vanderbilt University; Past President, Division of Clinical Psychology, American Psychological Association

～There is no doubt in my mind that going to a therapist may make a person feel worse and more unhappy. There may be numerous reasons for such an outcome. A prominent reason is that your friend may have consulted the "wrong" therapist, a person who may not be well trained and/or who has personal qualities that are detrimental. Perhaps your friend also had unrealistic expectations and was unmotivated to invest time and effort. There needs to be a good match between a patient and a therapist, and the secret is how to find out whether there is. At any rate, if a person does not feel better after a while, the situation requires close examination.

Largely in response to managed care, there is today a great deal of interest in empirical validation of therapeutic techniques. In my opinion, much nonsense is written on this topic: We should be more concerned about the therapist as a person than about the types of therapeutic techniques. My advice to a prospective patient would be to pay greatest attention to the reputation and overall competence of a therapist as well as to his or her kindness, caring, and commitment to the therapeutic tasks.

BOTTOM LINE

～There is no such thing in life as a magic pill or a miracle cure, and psychotherapy is no exception. As both experts note, some people may wind up in therapy with a person they just do not relate well with, or with whom they're just not comfortable. If so, psychotherapy can do more harm than good. Some people (and we've all met folks like this!) are determined to remain miserable, regardless of the cost. We've all encountered "life's victims," people who seem to stagger from one tragedy to the next, people who cannot get out of their own way. It would be a tall order for a therapist to radically change such an individual's nature. But for someone who needs help, has reasonable expectations, and wishes to be helped, therapy with the right person is one viable path to a solution. The bottom line is that therapy is *not* going to help everyone, and that therapy is not always the answer: It must be carefully considered, and a therapist must be carefully chosen if the process is to succeed.

Bigamy is having one husband too many.
Monogamy is the same.
　　—Erica Jong

　　The thing about having a baby is that thereafter you have it.
　　　　　　　　　　　　　　　　　　　　　　　　—Jean Kerr

When one has not had a father, one must create one.
　　—Friedrich Nietzsche

Problem 43

I HAVE JUST FOUND OUT THAT I HAVE accidentally gotten pregnant. I am a twenty-six-year-old graduate student, and the man who got me pregnant is my boyfriend of two years. I really care for him, but I do not feel ready for marriage. However, I do feel ready for parenthood. I would like to keep the baby and raise it alone, but I do not want to cut my boyfriend out of the child's life. What is the best thing I can do for my child in this situation? How can I ensure that my child will have financial support from its father? Should I get married just so that my child has an intact family, even though I fear the marriage may not last?

PROFESSIONAL OPINIONS

Roxanne Parrott, Ph.D., Author and Associate Professor,
Institute of Behavioral Research

➤ You should not get married just to have an intact family for your child. Nonetheless, your motives in this situation do require careful and honest consideration. You say that you feel ready for parenthood but not for marriage. Yet you want to know how to guarantee financial support from a man who may not feel ready to be either a parent or a husband. Your boyfriend deserves the same opportunity you have had to consider his options in this situation. Together, the two of you may come to some agreement regarding his involvement in this child's life, including financial support. You should not, however, make the decision to keep and raise a child based on whether the man you do not want to marry appears able to provide adequate financial support for you to raise the child.

Are you being honest when you say that the pregnancy was accidental, or that you do not want to get married? Or rather, is your fear that the marriage will not last based on personal observations and experiences outside the boundaries of your relationship with your boyfriend? Perhaps your feelings that you are ready to be a parent bespeak your longing for a committed relationship with your boyfriend, despite your recognition that he is not ready for marriage. If so, your pregnancy may make a difference in his feelings about the relationship and his commitment. Indeed, this may be exactly what you are secretly hoping for. But your more rational side suggests otherwise. At any rate, these are decisions to be made *after* talking with your boyfriend and not before.

Deb Poole, Ph.D., Author, Researcher, and Professor,
Central Michigan University

～You do not seem to have thought through your responsibilities to your boyfriend. Saying, "I do not want to cut my boyfriend out of the child's life," suggests that you would end the relationship if it were not for the baby, yet you also are contemplating marrying him. "How can I ensure that my child will have financial support from its father" sounds as though you envision your boyfriend as a twenty-year meal ticket rather than a co-parent who has rights, responsibilities, and decisions of his own to make. Now that you are pregnant, it is time to grow up and realize that the pregnancy not only gives you a child but draws you into a permanent relationship with your boyfriend as the father of that child. Your boyfriend, not you, will decide how involved he is in parenting the child, and the procedures in the states in which you both live will determine how easy or difficult it will be to demand support if he is less than thrilled about the pregnancy.

I suggest telling your boyfriend about your decision to keep the child and giving him time to think about how he envisions his role as a new father. It is not wise to marry under these circumstances, so consider continuing the relationship as it is for the time being and seeing what develops. I have several friends who married after their children were born, and they do not regret having let their relationships as couples develop gradually. Regardless of where the relationship goes, you have a responsibility to your child to treat its father with maturity and respect.

Alison Clarke-Stewart, Ph.D., Author, Editor, Researcher, and Professor, University of California

➤ Well that was really dumb of you! Why in this day and age would anyone, let alone a graduate student, "accidentally" get pregnant? Now it's time to grow up and stop acting dumb. I support your decision not to have an abortion. I believe that's the "right" thing to do. But be prepared for hard work ahead. (Oh, dear, I'm starting to sound like Dr. Laura Schlessinger!) Should you marry the guy who "got you pregnant" to give the baby an "intact" family, when you fear the marriage may not last? How would that provide an intact family? You really are dumb if that seems logical.

I think that the best thing is for you not to get married unless or until you are sure it is for a long, long time. (Are you certain you aren't just thinking of getting married for your own sake, so you won't be stigmatized as a single mom?) It would be great if that marriage could be to the baby's father, but if he's not "the one," then wait for someone you think is. This does not mean that the baby has to wait for a dad, though. If your boyfriend is willing, he should be involved in the baby's life—as much as possible, and forever, not just until your Mr.

Right comes along. Children benefit from a father's involvement with them in meaningful, day-to-day activities, and the best thing you can do is to encourage this kind of involvement from your boyfriend.

Invite your boyfriend to Lamaze classes and the birth. Let him spend time with you and the baby and with the baby alone. He'll be hooked. As for financial support, you can get a written financial commitment from your boyfriend that would be just as binding as a marriage certificate, I suppose. A father is legally bound to pay child support whether or not he is married to the child's mother in some states (check yours). But I think that the best way to ensure that your child has financial support from its father is by using a carrot (the baby), not a stick (threats of legal action). Good luck (and speaking of carrots, dry soda crackers are what I found best to combat those feelings of nausea that don't occur just in the mornings)!

BOTTOM LINE

➤ All three experts noted the immaturity and selfishness (of viewing the father as an economic resource without full consultative rights) of this woman. The bottom line is that this woman is feeling conflicted and unsure of what she wants, which is not surprising, given the discovery of an unplanned pregnancy. She does know that she wants this baby, however, and this change in her life requires her to think responsibly about her feelings about her boyfriend, his feelings about her, and their hopes and plans for the future. Several long talks are clearly called for.

This woman must also draw up a financial plan so that she budgets accordingly (babies are expensive!). She should consider all sources of income and ensure that sufficient funds will be available. The baby's father may wish to marry her, or he may not—in any case, the woman must, for the good of her child, do everything in her power to include this man in her baby's life *permanently*. Perhaps over the coming months her feelings and needs will become clearer. But she should do nothing to jeopardize what is good between her boyfriend and her, and should hope to build upon these feelings in the future. It is possible that these two will share in the joy of having this baby, and that the baby will be the best thing that ever happened to them. It is also possible that each will come deeply to resent the situation. Now is the time for them to take steps to make the former possibility a reality.

Sex is like air; it's not important unless you aren't getting any.
  —Anon.

   Women need a reason to have sex; men just need a place.
      —Anon.

Problem 44

I AM A FIFTY-ONE-YEAR-OLD MAN with three children, ages ten, twelve, and fifteen. My wife and I have been married for seventeen years. Our relationship has been completely devoid of sex for over four years, and nothing I have tried has helped. My wife just keeps telling me that ever since she became menopausal she has had no interest in sex. The doctor says she is experiencing normal feelings for a woman of her age with a busy schedule and career. But I am left feeling as though I may never have sex again, and I really miss it! Last week a close friend who lives about ninety minutes away suggested that I have an affair with her just for sex, and I am sorely tempted to do it. She and I have known one another for over twenty years, and we have always cared for one another, but we never dated. Now I must admit the prospect is very attractive. I do not want to divorce my wife over this problem because we have a good marriage and great kids, but I cannot keep on going without sex. What should I do?

PROFESSIONAL OPINIONS

Clyde Hendrick, Ph.D., Author, Researcher, and Professor,
Texas Tech University

➤ You need to try again! Your wife's doctor is wrong! It is not normal for a healthy woman to lose all interest in sex, even when she is menopausal. Has she had a complete physical exam, and is she on estrogen replacement therapy? Most important, have you sat down with her and told her how you feel, fully and completely? If she is willing, you both could benefit greatly from marriage counseling, preferably from someone who also does sex therapy. As for the possible affair, first think about your children. Do you really want to be that kind of role model for them? In time, they will find out. Such affairs often become gossiped about in the community. If all attempts at counseling fail and your wife continues to refuse sex, you might then discuss with her your desire for an outside affair. If she is agreeable, perhaps it would be acceptable. But be careful. What's supposed to be "pure sex" could become love. Then what would happen to your "good marriage"?

John Paul Gray, Ph.D., Clinical Psychologist, San Juan Capistrano, CA;
Past President, Orange County Psychological Association

➤ Try asking yourself if availability for sex was part of the marriage contract. Then ask yourself if the issues would be any different if *you* were unavailable for sex as a result of, say, a serious illness or being in a coma. Would it be acceptable to you for your wife to meet her sexual needs with an old friend? Last, ask yourself if the impulse of indulging your biological needs offsets the risk of devastating your wife and losing your own self-respect.

Your relationship is made of many facets, of which sex is an important one. Your task is to determine where sex ranks for you in your hierarchy. If it is true, as you say, that your relationship excels in many other areas of compatibility and you don't want a divorce, you need to stretch even more and try to seek reconciliation again (no one said relationships were easy). The first remedy is to talk to your wife, possibly using a professional to help you into some of the awkward areas. The basic questions are still the best starting point:

1. Let her know how important making love with her is to you and ask her what you may be doing, or not doing, that is turning her off. Get beyond your own defensiveness about this.

2. Ask her how to be a better lover to her, even if it sounds silly to you. Ask. Ask. Ask.

3. If her career and schedule wear her out, sneak her off for an evening or weekend rendezvous at a romantic place. You'd do that for an affair.

4. Ask her, and yourself, about any old anger or other baggage that might be getting in the way of relaxing. Remember, anger inhibits sexual response and vulnerability.

It is only human nature to feel strongly our own biological drives, such as sex, hunger, or the need for safety. But as an adult male, you've already learned that the uncensored indulgence of impulses can result in unpleasant consequences. The difference between humans and the other mammals is that we know we have consciousness, which is why we ascribe *responsibility* to us and *instinct* to the other animals. That translates into recognizing a feeling (impulse) and then making a decision on whether or not to act on it. Your dog or the garden-variety psychopath doesn't make such decisions.

The largest issue here has to do with the value you put on your commitment to fidelity, and has nothing to do with sex. To indulge your impulses, any impulses, that are contrary to your marital agreement devalues your relationship and whatever worth you put on your integrity. So look at your priorities in the relationship. Tune in to yourself enough to know what is important to you. Work on understanding your own value system.

Bottom Line

➤ Both experts urge the husband to be open and honest with his wife, and not to embark on a secret affair. The man in this situation is obviously feeling left out in the cold, and who can blame him? Four years is a long time to go without sex. He seems to have shown his wife understanding and kindness regarding her unwillingness, and he has not contemplated an affair until now. Clearly, he is desperate, and the prospect of a sex-only affair appeals to his animal urges.

The first thing he must do is tell his wife exactly how he is feeling, and possibly suggest to her an additional medical exam and some marriage counseling. He should present his wife with his dilemma—how to live without sex when a person deeply misses it—and ask her what she thinks he should do. It is essential that she be informed of just how upset he is. He should not state that he has been contemplating an affair, however, because this will be perceived as a threat. Plus, he is only contemplating the affair because he has been denied sex, and if his wife regained an interest in sex, he would undoubtedly no longer wish to stray.

The bottom line is that the wife must be nudged into taking at least some responsibility for this situation. If the husband has caused her to turn off, she must communicate this fact. If there is someone else, she must also communicate this—he has a right to know! If he tells his wife that he loves her very much and cherishes their life together but that he cannot go on like this, she may be willing to work on a solution. If not, he may wish to explore the possibility of a separation, unless he is able to quell his sexual needs. Sneaking around having extramarital sex while there are three children still living at home is not a good idea! People will find out, his marriage will erode further, his own sense of integrity will be tarnished, and the children will ultimately suffer for it. It would be better to deal with the situation directly and honestly, and if outside sex is necessary, confront this problem with his wife and compromise on a solution.

Confession is good for the soul only in the sense that
a tweed coat is good for dandruff.
    —Peter De Vries

The truth about a woman lies first and foremost in what she hides.
                                            —André Malraux

It is morally wrong to allow a sucker to keep his money.
    —Anon.

Problem 45

FOR EIGHT YEARS I HAVE HARBORED a deep, dark secret: My ex-husband is not the father of my son. If I tell him this, then I fear he will withdraw love and financial support from my son, whom he seems to love. Do I have a responsibility to tell my ex that he is not the biological father, even if there is a good chance that this will bring enormous suffering to my son?

PROFESSIONAL OPINIONS

Rowland Miller, Ph.D., Author, Researcher, and Professor,
Sam Houston State University

If you tell your ex-husband the truth, you will get your guilty burden off your chest, and you will be more fair to a man you have used dishonestly for several years. However, if you tell him, you will also rock (and quite possibly sink) a boat that is sailing along happily right now. You may rob both your ex-husband and your son of much of the joy they take in each other, and you will likely leave both of them less happy and worse off than they already are. My advice is: *Don't tell.* At this point, your honesty would be more self-serving than generous, doing others more harm than good. You should work hard to reduce your ex-husband's financial obligations to your son, and you should immediately write the truth into your will so that your son will always have an accurate genetic history if needed. But don't tell. Your dishonesty is regrettable, but others' happiness is more important than honesty here. Sometimes you have to live with a lie when the naked truth would be too ugly.

James Youniss, Ph.D., Author, Researcher, and Professor,
Catholic University of America
~ There is an Old World saying that one should never reveal an act of infidelity to a spouse—especially eight years later. But that folk wisdom needs to be balanced against the importance of this violation of marital trust. The inner turmoil of keeping this a secret is not likely to diminish with time. It is better to be honest and confront the consequences than to let doubt fester for a lifetime.

BOTTOM LINE

~ This is a tough one! As you can see, the experts disagree. This situation pits the rights of two people against one another. The ex-husband is supporting and caring for a child he does not even know is not his. If he *did* know the truth, he might choose immediately to terminate the relationship. Of course, he might choose to change nothing, because his love for the boy might outweigh his knowledge that it was someone else's sperm that created him. The truth might not matter to how he feels about the boy—although of course it would make him dislike the ex-wife even more! From the ex-husband's point of view, it does seem that he has the right to know. Plus, he may find out someday because of his son needing a medical procedure, having a blood test, or through countless other mechanisms. The matter of the boy's biological father is less important, since he has been out of the picture anyway and has made no contribution to the boy's welfare. However, the most important issue is the welfare of the child.

The ex-husband was having a sexual relationship with the woman, so in his mind, obviously, he could have been the boy's father. The boy thinks this is his father, and they have a good, ongoing relationship. It would crush the boy if the man he believes is his father were to withdraw love and support at this time. The two get along well, and the relationship seems to enrich both of them. What might this eight-year-old think if his father drew back upon learning the news? On the one hand, the boy might wonder if he did something to deserve abandonment by the man he thinks is his father. On the other hand, if he is told of his true paternity, he might think his mother is disgraceful. While it's true that the ex-husband may find out someday through other means that his son is not his biological child, for now, the best answer seems to be not to tell. Later, when the boy is older and more able to comprehend the complexities of the adult world, he will be better equipped to handle the shock of discovery.

However, this woman should do her best to maintain her son's standard of living without requiring financial support from the man, since in a sense she is using him by accepting it. In addition, the woman could write a detailed letter explaining the situation and her reasons for doing what she has done, perhaps getting it notarized to prove when it was written. She could later give this letter—or a copy of it—to her ex-husband and her son if the truth ever comes out. Perhaps this letter would help the man and boy to understand the soul-searching she has gone through. The bottom line is that the child's welfare should come first: The man is good to the boy, they love one another, and if it ain't broke, don't fix it.

Platonic friendship is the interval between
the introduction and the first kiss.
    —Anon.

            Human love is often but the encounter of two weaknesses.
                        —François Mauriac

Love lives on propinquity, but dies on contact.
    —Thomas Hardy

Problem 46

I AM A TWENTY-SEVEN-YEAR-OLD FEMALE business school student, and I have had the same best friend for the past six years: a man I met in college. We adore each other; there's nothing we can't talk about. We've each dated other people, but neither one of us has found Mr. or Ms. Right. Although we have never been involved romantically or sexually, lately I have begun to wonder whether we should try to have it all and develop a love relationship. We're not terribly attracted to one another physically, but we respect and admire each other for who we are. Am I silly to think it could become more? What should I do?

PROFESSIONAL OPINIONS

S. D. Boon, Ph.D., Researcher and Assistant Professor,
University of Calgary

Whether or not it's silly to think your friendship could become more depends heavily on your expectations (and those of your best friend, too) concerning the nature of love and the qualities both you and your friend desire in a romantic relationship. Although most popular views of love in our society presume that physical attraction, passion, and romance are defining features of romantic love, there are other criteria that might form the basis of a decision to start a love relationship. In my view, the friendship, admiration, and respect you and your best friend share are excellent foundations for such a relationship. Attraction based on physical appearance and/or passion may fade over time. Attraction based on mutual admiration and respect is more likely to endure.

However, if your ideal image of love is based on shared experiences of passion and physical attraction, you might be better off leaving things as they are. There are no guarantees that the liking you feel for your best friend will ever turn into passionate love. The two of you must decide how important physical attraction is to a relationship, and whether or not you require such attraction to "love" each other.

Robert Lemieux, Ph.D., Researcher and Assistant Professor,
Western Maryland College

～There is every reason to believe it can work. Your friendship is well established and would serve as a good foundation for a romantic relationship. The mere fact that you are wondering whether love could develop indicates that this friendship is capable of moving beyond friendship and into love. If he feels the same, then you should both pursue it.

As I see it, there are two sides to consider. On the positive side, you have a potential romantic partner with whom you are comfortable talking and sharing personal information. It also sounds as though you have common interests, and the length of your friendship suggests your commitment to each other. The only negative is the concern about having it not work out and altering a wonderful friendship. However, I believe the positives far outweigh the negatives. Once you get over the potential awkwardness of dating a friend, things should progress well. As for the importance of physical attractiveness, that depends upon your values. There are some who consider physical attractiveness to be a less important requirement for a good romantic relationship. Further, you may be surprised to realize how physically attractive a sensitive, caring lover can be.

BOTTOM LINE

～The experts see this one identically. The bottom line is that this woman has little to lose by opening a dialogue about the issue. She might approach her friend with a few questions, stating that lately she has been thinking that they have a very special relationship, and that perhaps it has been a mistake for them to seek lovers elsewhere instead of considering dating one another. If she acts tentatively in the discussion, the door will be open for her friend to disagree. The woman should be ready to hear that the man is not interested, and if he is not, she should accept this fact and not let her disappointment cloud the relationship. If he is not interested, she should continue the relationship for what it is: a rewarding friendship.

If, however, the man seems receptive, the woman might suggest they talk through some expectations and desires they have of a life mate. Perhaps they will discover yet more common ground. The lack of a fiery sexual attraction may not pose a problem, as long as neither individual craves sexual passion. Many people have learned that such intense attractions wane in time and can even lead to ill-formed decisions—otherwise known as thinking with the southern brain. And as the experts noted, a deep love relationship can bring two people to discover sexual attraction, particularly if there is intimacy and true friendship. Sex might in fact be better than either of them expects, precisely because they are so comfortable together. So this woman should test the waters with an open and honest discussion: She has little to lose, and potentially a lot to gain.

Depression was a very active state really. Even if you appeared to an observer to be immobilized, your mind was in a frenzy of paralysis. You were unable to function, but were actively despising yourself for it.
　　—Lisa Alther

Depression is the inability to construct a future.
　　—Rollo May

Depression is rage spread thin.
　　—Paul Tillich

Problem 47

I HAVE BEEN MARRIED FOR FIFTEEN YEARS to a wonderful woman, and for the first six years we had an idyllic relationship. Then, seemingly out of nowhere, she developed clinical depression. At first it was manageable, but as the years have passed her depressive episodes have lasted longer and have grown more severe. Now it is so bad that during her depressive periods she cannot even get out of bed, and she just cries and refuses to talk to me. When she is feeling good, she is still a terrific and warm person, but when the depression hits it is horrible. Other than this illness, there are no serious problems in our relationship, and the doctors have confirmed that I am doing nothing to cause her depression. Lately, I have begun to think that I should consider divorcing my wife and starting life again with someone new. I want to have a normal life, and I know that my wife will never get better. I have done everything I can, and I am just exhausted from nine years of trying to help. I would very much like to have a child, and this is impossible with my wife, as is any semblance of a normal life. What should I do?

PROFESSIONAL OPINIONS

Will Cupchik, Ph.D., Clinical Psychologist, Author, and Instructor,
University of Toronto

Since your wife's persisting depression may have an organic origin, I would recommend that you consider obtaining a full medical examination, possibly including a CAT scan as well as neurological and neuropsychological examinations. If the findings of this workup are negative, I would propose a full psychological assessment, including the Rorschach and Thematic Apperception Test, in order to ascertain whether there are some unconscious psychological issues that may be manifesting in her depression. I wonder what may have happened in your lives at about the time you say your spouse began being clinically depressed. Were there any major difficulties, or any illnesses or deaths in your families or among your friends? Sometimes even apparently innocuous events in one's current life can trigger deep-seated emotional reactions pertaining to events that happened much earlier in one's life, especially in childhood. Marital therapy might also uncover some heretofore ignored issues. Should all the above efforts prove to be of no help, and should you decide to separate, being involved with a marital therapist could provide a supportive environment to help your wife deal with this new situation and possibly prevent a worsening of her depression.

Diana Odom Gunn, Ph.D., Author, Researcher, and Instructor,
University of Kansas

～It sounds like you remain very much in love with your wife but you loathe her depression. Are you willing to try something new for one year only? If so, I recommend that you pursue as normal a life as you wish you were living. It may be possible to keep your wonderful wife but divorce her depression. You seem to have been trying for a long time to fix your wife's depression. Instead, turn your energies on yourself. Fix your own life and you may be amazed at the improvement in your marriage! Join community groups, develop hobbies, make friends, and go to parties, even though you must do these things alone. You need to develop interests that do not involve your wife. This change in you won't help your wife's condition, but it will change your experience of her condition. Building a life for yourself will make your response to your wife's feelings less extreme, and you will find her condition much easier for you to tolerate.

Filling up your own life may also make you a better companion for her by providing you with new insights and experiences to share with her at home, thus enriching the good times you have together. If you do this for one year, I think you will find yourself much happier about your life and also about your marriage. At that point, you may wish to reconsider having a child from your new perspective on life. If you do not feel things have improved after one year, go forward with the divorce knowing you've tried everything. Then use your newly established friendships and interests to help you adjust to the end of your marriage.

BOTTOM LINE

⌐ First, this man must ensure that he has done everything possible to provide his wife with excellent medical advice and care. Second, he must ensure that he has done what he can to address and improve any behaviors of his own that may have contributed to her depression. He should ask himself, How do things appear from his wife's side, and how does she see the situation? If she truly sees herself as a victim of an organic disorder, and if she believes he has done everything he can to be supportive, then he can at least know that his wife sees him as not contributing to the problem. If she does see him as a partial cause of the problem, he must deal with these issues.

Once he has gotten to the point at which he has done everything he can, he must ask himself whether his life is tolerable. If the answer is no, and if he has spent nine years trying to help his wife without success, he has the right to move on and seek a more fulfilling life with someone else. In the event that he chooses to leave, he must help his wife both emotionally and financially to weather this transition. Perhaps he could talk to her family and enlist their support. Even if they resent him for considering leaving his wife, he may be able to help them understand why he feels so desperate and how empty his life is. If her family can help by being supportive of her, the transition might be less stressful. This man owes his wife everything he can do to try to help her, and he owes her decent and fair treatment. But he does not owe her being a captive to her mental illness for the rest of his life

When I hear somebody sigh that "life is hard," I'm always tempted to ask . . . "compared to what?"
    —Sidney Harris

Little privations are easily endured when the heart is better treated than the body.
    —Jean-Jacques Rousseau

Love doesn't grow on trees like apples in Eden—It's something you have to make and you must use your imagination to make it too, just like anything else. It's all work, work.
    —Joyce Cary

Problem 48

EVER SINCE MY WIFE GAVE BIRTH to our first child, it's like I was left out in the cold. My wife used to be very affectionate toward me, but now she is distant and spends all her time and energy on taking care of the baby (aged five months). We haven't started having sex again since the birth, and worse yet, my wife doesn't even hug or kiss me or tell me she loves me, unless it is to repeat the words back after I say them first. When she is with our son, I see all the energy and love she is capable of giving—and that used to be mine. Am I being selfish? Is her behavior normal, and will things change? What should I do?

PROFESSIONAL OPINIONS

Connie Schick, Ph.D., Author, Researcher, and Professor, Bloomsburg University

Both of you are suffering from the myth that parenting is blissful. You have realistic (and common) feelings: Why isn't this bliss? (resentment), Why does she ignore me? (jealousy, anger, fear of rejection), Will it ever be better? (despair). She has not deserted you; she is caught in the stress trap—physically run down from tending the baby and losing personal time, worried she won't be a good mother, and resentful that it isn't easy and natural. Her stress is also responsible for loss of sexual interest; the adrenals are active in producing sexual and stress chemicals in women, and right now stress is winning! I suggest you talk, encouraging an exchange of doubts and feelings. By reassuring each other and sharing expectations, you will both live through it and lay a foundation for discussing the other problems parenting will bring as your child grows. You might also enjoy participating in a well-baby parenting group. It will help to know that women's least happy time in marriage is before the child starts school. However, men and women report being most happy when all children have left the nest, so if you were happy before, the best is yet to come!

Karen Fingerman, Ph.D., Researcher and Assistant Professor, Pennsylvania State University

➤ Your feelings are normal. Most couples find it stressful adapting to the permanent "company" in their lives after the birth of a first child. Your challenge is figuring out how to remain a couple and be parents simultaneously. It sounds like you are focusing on the first issue, and your wife is focusing on the second. Schedule a time when you can get away from your child and enjoy each other's company. Talk about adult feelings—tell your wife how much you love her, and bring up your concerns. Perhaps you can take a more active role as a parent. When babies are this age, they are responsive and cuddly. By taking over some of the child care, you'll see why your wife is so engrossed and your jealousy may subside. (I bet your baby is gorgeous, a budding genius, and superstar—at least in your eyes.) If the new mother gets some respite from the demands she faces, hopefully she'll have the energy to think about other things (including you). Enjoy your child and slowly encourage your wife to spend more time as a couple. Expect this adjustment to take a while but to be worth it in the end.

BOTTOM LINE

~According to these experts, the bottom line is that the man must be understanding and supportive of his wife, but at the same time he must gently make his needs known to her without placing too much pressure on her. First, he must recognize that his wife's behavior is completely normal. Nearly all women experience such feelings, and often sexual desire does not return right away following childbirth. The wife may be exhausted and stressed out. If the husband takes on some of the burdens of child rearing and provides his wife with release time to spend shopping, exercising, or with her own friends— or just sleeping for more than two hours at a time—he may find her energy starts to return, and her focus starts to expand beyond simply the baby.

It might be helpful for the wife to schedule several sessions with a therapist familiar with postpartum depression. Also, vigorous exercise programs have been shown to help decrease depression and increase energy. If the husband gently makes his needs known in a nonthreatening way while showing his wife that he understands what she is feeling, he may find that over time she becomes more receptive to his needs. He is not being selfish per se, but he is being shortsighted. This woman has gone through the traumas of pregnancy and has given birth to his child, and he should cut her some slack.

Each [of my wives] was jealous and resentful of my preoccupation with business. Yet none showed any visible aversion to sharing in the proceeds.
—J. Paul Getty

I can't be a rose in any man's lapel.
—Margaret Trudeau

Problem 49

WHEN I MARRIED MY WIFE, who is fifteen years my junior, she was thrilled—she went from living at the near-poverty level to having a lovely home and a stable life. My wife is a beautiful woman whom my friends have referred to as my middle-age "trophy." I explained to my wife ahead of time exactly what our life together would be like—traveling, corporate parties, entertaining, and so on. At first she was excited and loved getting dressed up and entertaining my colleagues and friends. But now she is argumentative and mopes around the house, saying that her life is empty and that she "needs more." I am clueless: What I promised her is exactly what she said she wanted and what she got! What should I do now?

PROFESSIONAL OPINIONS

Cynthia S. Burnley, Ph.D., Researcher and Associate Professor, East Tennessee State University

Being rescued from near poverty and offered an entertaining, comfortable, and stable lifestyle may have been very appealing to your wife initially. You have referred to your colleagues and friends. What about *her* colleagues and friends—

has she maintained contact since she has been married? You did not say if she had moved away from a job, family, or friends to marry you. She may feel empty because everything in her life revolves around one person. Perhaps your friends are accurate and she is a "trophy" wife. She may need to pursue interests of her own (e.g., employment, friends, organizations) and not let her life revolve only around you. If so, be ready to share her life and provide mutual support in entertaining her colleagues and friends. You will find your wife and relationship enriched in the process as you truly share your lives as a couple.

Eric Dubow, Ph.D., Author, Researcher, and Professor,
Bowling Green State University

— This situation is going to require some flexibility on your part if you want this relationship to last. However, I'm not sure this is going to be easy for you. First, you seem to enjoy that your friends refer to your wife as your "middle-age 'trophy.'" Second, you say that your wife "loved getting dressed up and entertaining" *your* colleagues and friends, almost implying that this is her responsibility—but what about *her* friends? Third, you say, "I explained to my wife ahead of time exactly what our life together would be like," suggesting to me that you did not (and do not) perceive that interpersonal relationships change over time. And fourth, you are "clueless" as to why she "needs more." So you may not be ready to make the important changes in your attitudes and behavior for this relationship to continue.

You must be open to understanding your wife's current needs. You must realize that people grow, especially when given opportunities and resources previously unavailable to them. Does she now want to work outside of the home, start a family, pursue her own interests, have input into (or control over) major and minor decisions in your lives? If you cannot get to the bottom of these issues with her, either because you are closed to change or because she has learned not to upset your apple cart, it's worth seeking professional help.

BOTTOM LINE

◆ Both experts detected the one-sided, egocentric way this husband describes his wife. This man is in a tough situation. It's clear that he plucked his wife out of her near-poverty-level existence and inserted her into his life like a new, expensive possession, expecting her to be happy and not to complain. How selfish of him! And as far as she is concerned, it is tough to imagine why she would have married someone if she was not truly in love with him. If she *was* in love—and not simply seeking financial salvation—then there must have been some basis for this love. Perhaps she later found out that the man was not who she thought he was at first. Perhaps he learned that she was not going to be satisfied indefinitely with being his trophy. In any case, their situation will require a lot of work if they are going to create a happy marriage out of what they now have.

First off, this woman must build a life of her own. She must pursue and develop her own interests, go to school, start a business, whatever. She must demand respect from him and treatment as his equal. If he refuses, the marriage is doomed. If, however, he is a big enough person to come to view his trophy wife as a real flesh-and-blood woman whom he can respect and admire, and whom he treats as an equal, there is hope. Some counseling might help here. But really, it comes down to whether the woman is a big enough person to build a life for herself on her own terms, and whether the man is a big enough person to stop thinking of his wife as a pretty young toy he takes to parties, and instead as a worthwhile person deserving of his affections and respect.

*We sleep in separate rooms, we have dinner apart,
we take separate vacations—we're doing everything
we can to keep our marriage together.*
—Rodney Dangerfield

*One half the world cannot understand
the pleasures of the other half.*
—Jane Austen

Problem 50

MY BOYFRIEND AND I HAVE ALMOST completely nonoverlapping hobbies—he likes outdoor sports and rough activities, while I enjoy crafts and indoor stuff. Fortunately, we have enough in common, like enjoying movies and restaurants, so that we have plenty of things to do when we're together. But my friends think it's weird that we spend our days doing separate activities—I go to tag sales, museums, and shops, while he goes sea kayaking or skiing. Each of us has a circle of friends we share our hobbies with. My friends say I should find someone with whom I have more interests in common—but I think this isn't that important. Who's right?

PROFESSIONAL OPINIONS

*Gail Carr Feldman, Ph.D., Clinical Psychologist, Author, and Assistant
Professor, University of New Mexico*

You're both right! If it's true that you and your boyfriend "have plenty of things to do" when you're together and that you enjoy one another's company, there's certainly nothing "weird" or wrong about that. And yet, when your friends say you should find someone with whom you have more in common, I suspect they are considering the future and the possibility of marriage. While enjoying someone's company on occasion doesn't require you to have similar interests or values, a potential marriage partnership calls for a full inventory of shared interests, values, and goals for the future.

If you decide to evaluate your relationship for marriage potential, I suggest that you write down a list of goals—what you'd like your life to be like in five years, and maybe in ten years, in the following four areas: (1) career and financial; (2) relationships and family; (3) pastimes, indoor and outdoor hobbies, and activities (including travel); and (4) psychological and spiritual development. Invite your boyfriend to make his own lists. As you both work on these thoughts and ideas, you'll be evolving a sense about whether the two of you could be committed partners over the long haul. In the meantime, just enjoy each other.

Ladd Wheeler, Ph.D., Author, Researcher, Professor, and University of Rochester; Past President of Society for Personality and Social Psychology

➤ As long as you have things you enjoy doing together, having different hobbies is fine. I'd suggest that you make an effort to understand and appreciate one another's hobbies, however, so that after a day of museums and kayaking, you can share your fun.

BOTTOM LINE

➤ It seems that couples these days do everything together, but this is not necessarily the only or the best way to build a relationship. Having separate hobbies and circles of friends can be healthy. Couples in such relationships always have new experiences to share with one another and new things to discuss. What is essential is that *both* partners agree that what they are doing is what they want. If one person is secretly—or openly—anxious about the other's activities or time spent with others, the couple is in for trouble. If there is a balance in which both partners view the world the same way, things can work out well.

An important thing for this couple to remember is to maintain an atmosphere in which both people could share their feelings if they felt they were getting too little time or attention. The only other consideration applies if this couple starts contemplating a lifelong commitment. In this case, they must be sure to talk through their expectations about the amount of time they will spend together so there are no surprises. Sometimes, what works when people are dating no longer works after marriage: Expectations can change. The one thing not to worry about is the opinions of friends, as long as the woman and man in the relationship are happy. For many decades men and women lived largely separate lives within committed relationships, and these relationships were often very successful. The bottom line is that there is more than one way to create a happy relationship.

In real love you want the other person's good.
In romantic love you want the other person.
—Margaret Anderson

When success comes in the door, it seems,
love goes out the window.
—Dr. Joyce Brothers

Problem 51

LAST NIGHT MY WIFE ANNOUNCED that she was offered a fabulous job in a city two hours away from where we now live, and that she accepted the offer (which she had to do or else lose the position to another applicant). When we'd discussed this possibility in the past, I had remained mute, not wanting to start an argument. But now it's a done deal as far as she's concerned, and she intends to sell our house and move, taking our two children with her. The trouble is that I like my job, and I like living where we now live. It's true that we moved here ten years ago for my job, and that she took a job she didn't like very much—but I didn't realize she would eventually want "equal time." Now I feel broadsided, and the most sympathy she's showing is to call real estate agents. What should I do?

PROFESSIONAL OPINIONS

Kimberly Hause-Swales, Ph.D., Researcher and Professor,
University of Houston

➤ There are two issues at the heart of this conflict. First, there is a severe lack of communication in this marriage. The most important thing one should always do in these situations is *communicate.* Since you did not express your feelings to your wife during past discussions, she might not have any idea how you feel about her new position or the move. Ideally, you would have talked openly before she accepted the position. However, you still need to communicate your frustration and dismay to her now. If you silence these feelings, you might boil inside with resentment. Furthermore, you and your wife should make an agreement to have open and honest discussions before making any major decisions in the future.

Second, it seems that you think it is acceptable for a wife to move for her husband's career but the reverse is unacceptable. Your wife made a similar sacrifice for you ten years ago. Why wouldn't she expect the same support in return? I wonder if you think that your career is more important than your wife's. Marriage is often about compromise, and it seems this time it is your turn to give in.

Vickie Harvey, Ph.D., Author, Researcher, and Assistant Professor,
John Carroll University

➤ A major family decision was made without the entire family's input. This is not usually the best way to make decisions that affect other people's lives. Your wife's announcement at first appears to be a decision that was reached without mutual discussion. However, your choice to remain "mute" indicates that the topic had been open for discussion and your wife took the more active role. You declined the opportunity for input, leaving the responsibility in her hands. Assuming full responsibility for the decision, she weighed the options, choose a fabulous job two hours away, and now intends to sell the house and move, taking the children with her. Although you gave limited input into the job decision itself, you still have the opportunity to contribute to related decisions and to explore other possibilities, such as her moving alone and your staying, both of you moving to a town halfway between your jobs and both commuting, or your commuting from the city where her job is. There are still possibilities that need to be decided upon, and you need to be a participant in those decisions. The important thing is that you become an active member and not a silent, brooding partner who is unwilling to speak up during the discussion period but then wants a full voice after things have been decided.

BOTTOM LINE

The bottom line is that the husband was wrong to delay the discussion out of his fear of starting an argument—but his wife was even more wrong to have decided unilaterally to move the family without hearing out her husband. This woman is acting as if she is an independent agent. If this is how she feels, she may want a divorce or a de facto divorce or separation anyway, and she may not care what her husband thinks. She may feel deeply resentful about the sacrifices of having to stay in a less-than-optimal job for the past ten years because of him. Now she sees it as her turn to get her way, and she is moving, with or without him.

What this man must decide is whether his two children are worth the sacrifice of his job and current life. If he can relocate for his children and not be unhappy, then he should go. If he cannot, he should tell his wife he is unwilling to give up his current job and see what type of compromise they can arrive at. Perhaps he can keep an apartment in the area near his job and commute to spend three days a week with his children, even working one day a week at home. Perhaps his wife would be willing to buy a new house at an intermediate position so that they could live together but both would have to commute one hour. Or perhaps his wife would agree to allow the children to live with him in their current home, and she could move and get the apartment near her new job and commute (although this does seem unlikely!).

One thing's clear: This marriage is and has been in big trouble for a long time. The wife should never have made the ten-year sacrifice if she was going to resent her husband for it. Now she is fighting back. She has a right to expect equal time, however, and if he does not choose to support her, this couple is probably better off apart. Children can perceive an atmosphere of resentment, so remaining in a day-to-day committed relationship may not be the best solution for this family. If there is deep unhappiness and resentment, the man and woman should admit it and get counseling to work out a mutually agreeable solution that would cause the least damage to the children.

Religion is a great force—the only real motive force in the world; but you must get at a man through his own religion, not through yours.
—George Bernard Shaw

The fact that we are human beings is infinitely more important than all the peculiarities that distinguish us.
—Simone de Beauvoir

Problem 52

I AM A THIRTY-ONE-YEAR-OLD RELIGIOUS Jewish woman who has fallen in love with a thirty-five-year-old Catholic man! I never would have thought it was possible given my upbringing, but he and I met at work and we have developed a very deep bond. He is a terrific person with a lot of character and a responsible position. He is not particularly religious (he doesn't go to church every week), but he will not consider converting. I want to marry and have a family, and I believe he wants the same thing. My parents think he's a nice guy, but they are adamant that I not marry him because of our religious differences. His parents don't seem to mind that he's dating a Jewish woman, although they are religious Catholics and do not support the idea of conversion either. Am I being unwise to move forward with this man? Can I expect a stable marriage and family life despite our religious differences?

PROFESSIONAL OPINIONS

James L. Johnson, Ph.D., Researcher, Marriage Counselor, and Clinical Psychologist, Claremont, CA

People who marry thinking love will conquer all are usually disappointed. The real thinking is, "Because my partner loves me (or we love each other), he/she will let me have my way." Of course you can see the problem if both, with competing ideas, are expecting love will "give me my way." In this case, the more valued religion is, the more important it is that the couple's religious direction be decided upon before marriage. A corollary issue concerns the in-laws. The more important in-laws are to the couple, the more important it is to come to a consensus about their religious direction, taking in-laws into consideration.

Usually, religious differences are most acutely felt when children arrive. I would ask the couple, in what religion are you going to raise your children? These two people are not ready for marriage if they cannot find a solution satisfying to both of them that takes into consideration its possible ramifications for the in-laws.

Deb Poole, Ph.D., Author, Researcher, and Professor,
Central Michigan University

◣Marrying against your parents' wishes will be emotionally difficult, but it will be equally difficult to find another man about whom you care as much. Start by talking to your parents about what their *specific* concerns and disappointments are. Are they worried that your children will not be raised in the faith? Are they concerned that your household will not continue the traditions your parents value? Because your children will be Jewish regardless of your husband's faith, your parents might soften once they have an understanding of how this new man might affect their lives and the lives of their grandchildren. In any "mixed" marriage, it is also helpful if each partner invests some energy in learning about the history and traditions of the other family. Most parents enjoy telling the stories of their youth; it's likely that your parents will warm up considerably if your partner shows an interest by having read a bit about your traditions, then inviting your parents to talk with a few sincere questions (e.g., "Tell me about what your family did on Rosh Hashanah when you were little").

BOTTOM LINE

➤ Both of these experts raise an important point. If a couple cannot agree on which religion they will raise children in, or on the importance of having in-laws play a role in family life, they are not ready for an interfaith marriage—or for any marriage, for that matter, given how important it is to work out ahead of time issues involving children and in-laws. Yet the two people in this situation deeply love each other, and they must bear in mind that love this deep comes along only rarely. So a decision to terminate the relationship because of religious differences will inevitably cause both partners to wonder if they were somehow cheated by the strength of their parents' religious feelings.

This woman and man need to go away alone and talk over their positions, and what their feelings mean for them now and later. If religion means so much to them that they are willing to sacrifice their future together, they should admit this and terminate the relationship. However, it seems that neither partner is deeply immersed in religion himself or herself. If this is the case, they should consider telling their parents to butt out and admit publicly and privately their lack of religious commitment. In short, they should stop living for their parents and start living for themselves, whatever this means.

Love is the only game in which two can play and both can lose.
—Anon.

Patience has its limits, take it too far, and it's cowardice.
—George Jackson

Problem 53

MY WIFE HAS A HABIT OF WITHHOLDING sex whenever she is angry with me. Sometimes her anger is justified and sometimes it is not, but her reaction is always to draw away from me for days. I have tried talking with her, and her perspective is that she should not be forced to have sex when she does not feel like it, regardless of the reason. She says that she will have sex only when she is capable of enjoying it, and that it is wrong of me to assume that just because I want sex, she should submit. I believe that it is reasonable for a person to expect sex from his or her spouse as long as that person isn't ill, and I think it is wrong for her to use sex as a tool to punish me. Who is right?

PROFESSIONAL OPINIONS

Susan S. Hendrick, Ph.D., Clinical Psychologist, Researcher, Marriage and Family Therapist, and Professor, Texas Tech University

➤You are both right—and you are both wrong. At its best, sex is intimate, companionable, and pleasurable. It is not meant to be used as a weapon and withheld as a form of partner punishment. In withholding sex, your wife is also withholding herself, and when this happens, you both lose out. She needs to be more direct with you, telling you what she is angry about and clearly asking for changes in the relationship. However, sex is also meant to be freely given; it is not a debt that one partner "owes" to the other. Good sex—and a good relationship—is based on communication and negotiation, not "submission." If you can begin to view sex as something desired rather than demanded, your love life is likely to improve. Sex can be hard to talk about, but talking is what you and your wife need to do! So make a date for a walk on the beach or in the park, where you may be a bit more relaxed as you talk about your relationship. Then walk and talk and let nature take its course.

Miles Patterson, Ph.D., Author, Editor, Researcher, and Professor, University of Missouri

━ The question "Who is right?" implies that assigning responsibility for this conflict will somehow lead to a solution. The first concern here is to resolve the problem that precipitated your wife's anger, whether it was justified or not. It's likely that her anger and your response to it affect not only sexual intimacy but other areas of your relationship as well. For example, on both sides, the negative feelings associated with the conflict over sex can undermine routine cooperation and goodwill on other issues. Furthermore, even if you "succeed" in pressuring your wife into having sex because it is her responsibility, the long-term costs are likely to outweigh the short-term benefits. No one likes to be forced into a course of action. She will resent being pressured into having sex, just as you resent her withholding it. If you can address the source of the anger, the chances for a mutual, cooperative resolution will increase.

Bruce E. Wampold, Ph.D., Author, Editor, Researcher, and Professor, University of Wisconsin

━ Fortunately, neither of you is right. This is one of those situations in which both you and your wife look as if you are in the right, but only from your own perspectives. From your perspective, it seems unreasonable that your wife withholds sex from you as a form of punishment. From your wife's perspective, it seems unreasonable that you would expect her to have sex when she is not feeling close to you. What you and your wife need is a way to resolve your disagreements before they build into resentments. You also need opportunities to feel intimate without having to check first whether some resentments have built up. I suggest that the two of you agree not to have sex for a few weeks and to spend that time enjoying each other, pledging that you will resolve conflictual issues as they arise. If you cannot do this on you own, I suggest the assistance of a psychologist or counselor.

BOTTOM LINE

~ If this woman is using sex in a preprogrammed, transactional manner to manipulate and control her husband, she is wrong and unfair. If, however, she is simply angry, upset, and miserable for a while, it is reasonable that she would not want to have sex. She would not be able to enjoy it at such times, and she would become angry at her husband for insisting on sex, which would end up worsening their problems. The issue is whether she is selecting sex as a calculated tool that she can use to control her husband.

For example, a woman who says, "I will withhold sex until he agrees to go to where I want to go this year on vacation," is avoiding the real problem. In this case, the woman should insist on a solution that addresses the real issue (such as how the couple negotiate their leisure time). Withholding sex will only make the man angry, cause more distance in the relationship, and wear down any bond that exists between them.

If his wife is angry and upset, he should try to work out what is really bothering her, and hopefully this will loosen her up. If she is using sex as a calculated effort to control, they should seek professional help so that she becomes aware of her transactional nature ("I give you sex only when you give me what I want"). But, as all three experts point out, the man is wrong to expect sex whenever he wants it unless the other person is ill—marriage does not give a person this right in any practical sense. How can he expect an act based on intimacy and trust to be performed by a partner who feels alienated and possibly even betrayed? The bottom line is that this couple must figure out what is really bothering this woman.

I felt it shelter to speak to you.
    —Emily Dickinson

It seems to me that trying to live without friends is like milking a bean to get cream . . . it is a whole lot of trouble, and then not worth much after you get it.
    —Zora Neale Hurston

Problem 54

I AM A PROFESSIONAL WOMAN in my midthirties, married for nearly four years. My husband is a computer analyst and a terrific guy in almost every way, with one major exception. He wants to come between me and my female friends. He acts jealous of my relationship with these women, whom I have known since college. These women and I have become a support group for each other's professional development and aspirations. When I return from our weekly group dinner, he gives me the "third degree," asking about where we went, what we did, and exactly what we talked about so late. He says *I* am *his* best friend and confidante, and he doesn't understand why these women are so important to me. It drives me crazy! I love this man dearly, but his jealousy and desire to control my friendships are driving a wedge between us. How should I handle this?

PROFESSIONAL OPINIONS

Ralph B. Hupka, Ph.D., Author, Researcher, and Professor, California State University

◣ You and your husband have different views about the obligations husbands and wives have to each other. Bring these unspoken expectations into the open and discuss them. This will defuse the flame they ignite in both of you. It helps to realize that in America, with its many different cultures, there are conflicting ideas of how wives and husbands should relate. Several hundred years ago, your husband's questions would have been interpreted by the European settlers as a sign of love and a commitment to defend the honor of the family. Even today a substantial proportion of Americans would consider you unreasonable for demanding to eat dinner with friends once a week. Their reasoning would be that marriage involves a commitment to each other. You are spouses, not roommates. Another issue worth discussing with your husband is the tendency of American men to make friends of their wives, whereas women prefer friendships outside of marriage. He's satisfied with you and can't understand why you are not satisfied with him. Reassure him of your love, and let him know daily that he is a terrific guy.

Joseph P. Bush, Ph.D., Author, Researcher, and Clinical Psychologist, The Fielding Institute

➤ You say that your husband "wants to come between me and my female friends." Are you sure this is the real motive behind his jealous behavior? It would be wise to explore carefully the reasons for his jealousy. Is it possible that he is possessive of you or threatened by your outside friendships? Or might it be that he is envious—wanting something like you have for himself as well? I wonder what it is that he feels he is missing. He says that you are his best friend and confidante. Is he yours? If not, it is not surprising that he is jealous—but this is not romantic jealousy. If this is the case, the two of you need to make some decisions. If he wants a closer friendship with you, are you willing to work toward this? Perhaps your husband also needs some close friendships outside of your relationship but does not know how to find them.

Alternatively, perhaps your husband is feeling a lack of intimacy in your relationship and is attributing this to your group of female friends. This is something you would need to explore, both individually and together. Finally, there may be differences between the two of you in terms of your definitions of marriage and your expectations regarding outside relationships. Your marriage is still young, and you may yet have some things to learn about what each other wants in this respect.

BOTTOM LINE

～ Each expert notes that this woman has a serious problem, and that she is justifiably angry, but they also note that she must approach her husband with kindness and warmth instead of with rigidity and demandingness. Concrete suggestions include these: First, she can try inviting her husband along to an evening with her female friends—assuming that these friends also invite their partners. Second, she can encourage her husband to make new friendships, perhaps in the context of taking up a hobby, that will involve him with others outside of marriage. Her husband may become more relaxed about her activities if he starts having opportunities to participate in similar activities on his own, especially on her nights out. Also, the wife can suggest that the husband ask his male friends at work, for example, about the activities they participate in without their wives, and vice versa. Perhaps appreciating that going out without one's spouse is customary will help the husband relax.

If the problem has become too entrenched, and if her husband is unwilling to budge, the wife might suggest a few counseling sessions to get at what is bothering him. Is this man overly needy in other areas? Why is he so threatened? Does this man worry that his wife is revealing private details of their marriage to her friends? If so, some reassurance may help; and inviting all the women's partners to join the women on some of their nights out might demystify for the male partners what is going on. If the husband needs more, she can definitely recommend therapy. No marriage can take the place of all outside friendships, nor should it be expected to. Just because a spouse has close outside friends—of either gender—does not mean something is wrong. The bottom line is that the husband has to become more flexible, and the wife has to reassure him and nudge him in this direction, either on her own or with the help of a marriage counselor.

A father gives his daughter the sense of what her bargaining position with all men will be.
—Shirley Abbott

He that with the daughter win
Must with the mother first begin.
—Seventeenth-century English proverb

Problem 55

My WIFE AND I CONTINUALLY argue about the benefit of forcing our daughter to compete in sporting events. If we left it to our daughter, she would decline all invitations to participate in team sports, and most social invitations, too. She is shy and tends to avoid people she doesn't know well. I feel that we shouldn't push her into such situations until she feels ready. But my wife says she will miss out on many events that are entertaining and that may help her actualize her potential, and forcing her to accept invitations will help her feel more comfortable in social settings. Who is right?

PROFESSIONAL OPINIONS

Valerie Cole, Ph.D., Clinical Psychologist, Researcher, and Assistant Professor, St. John Fisher College

My suggestion is for you and your wife to stop arguing with each other and start listening to your daughter. It doesn't matter which one of you is right; what matters is how your daughter is feeling. Talk with her, and find out what she really is concerned about. Perhaps her motivation to stay out of social situations has nothing to do with being shy. It is possible that she feels that no matter what she does, it will never be enough to make people like her. After all, that's her situation right now at home. Whether she participates or doesn't participate, one of her parents is not going to approve and will be unhappy with her. If she feels this way, forcing her into social situations is not going to help her feel more comfortable. Perhaps if both you and your wife express your real concern and love for her, and listen deeply to her concerns, she will begin to understand that her presence and her feelings are important to others, and that people enjoy being with her—things she's probably not feeling right now. You may find that she will then want to become more social.

Mary Lyn Huffman, Ph.D., Author and Visiting Assistant Professor, University of Sewanee

～I don't think the main issue is who is right or wrong, the husband or wife. I rather think the two parents need to think about their motivations for reacting one way or the other, and then decide as a united front what should be done. Children and teenagers can actualize their potential in many settings other than in direct competition. For example, the daughter might feel more comfortable or excited about learning a musical instrument instead of being in athletic competitions. You need to focus on her becoming socially adjusted with others her age.

Since her age is not given, I will respond as if she were a young child. If she is elementary-school aged, you as parents are more responsible for her activities, so you should expose her to different activities involving peers (e.g., art classes, musical lessons, individual and team sports). When she becomes a teenager, she will be able to dive more specifically into an activity she enjoys. I do not think she should be forced to be involved in a competitive sport.

I also do not believe that the daughter will seek social situations when she is ready. (This is the perspective of the maturational theory of development.) It seems that this child is introverted and will not seek others out. I also do not think that children know what is best for them at all times. That is why development takes place in the context of families. Thus, the parents need to realize that they should encourage their daughter in many activities so that she tries on different hats socially and sees which ones fit most comfortably.

The child has probably inherited this personality/temperament from her parents (or extended family), so the parents should rethink their childhoods and remember how they wished similar situations would have been handled. There might be things their parents did that merit repeating with a quiet or socially withdrawn child. The parents might also benefit from seeking the advice of other parents with similar children and finding out what might aid their child's social adjustment. In conclusion, the parents must not make the child feel ashamed or inadequate because she is more introverted.

BOTTOM LINE

⌖ As parents, this man and his wife wish to give their daughter the best possible start in life, and who can blame them? The trouble is that he and his wife disagree, although both have the child's best interest at heart. Step number one is for the parents to halt all disagreement in front of their child, who must feel like a yo-yo at this point—damned if she does and damned if she doesn't. Next, the parents must work out between themselves a compromise that they can both live with, and both must agree to enforce this decision. Ideally, the daughter's input would be heard and given a high weight in this decision-making process. If the daughter were doing poorly in school, or were engaging in risky behavior, the parents would have a legitimate right to use force to ensure her compliance. But in this case we are talking about extracurricular activities that are supposed to be fun! If the child does not enjoy these activities, the mother should ask herself why she is pushing her. Is it to fulfill the mother's own needs? If so, this is unhealthy.

Perhaps the child could suggest one activity that she would enjoy. Other than this, she could be allowed to participate in less highly social situations, in which she would feel more comfortable. Each child is unique, and just because the mother may have been Ms. Sociability does not mean this is right for her daughter. The bottom line is that the mother should back off and stop creating major arguments; this issue is just not worth it. The father should work things out with the mother out of earshot of the child, even if this means getting some counseling to work through the mother's reasons for wanting to push the child.

It's hard to raise sons, and much harder to raise daughters.
    —Sholem Aleichem

The role of a retired person is no longer to possess one.
    —Simone de Beauvoir

Enjoy what you can and endure what you must.
    —Johann Wolfgang von Goethe

Problem 56

I AM A SIXTY-TWO-YEAR-OLD WOMAN married for thirty-six years to a sixty-five-year-old man. One of my grown children, my twenty-eight-year-old daughter, has moved back into my house, bringing her two young children. Her marriage failed after her husband became abusive and alcoholic. Financial concerns have forced her to dramatically scale back her standard of living; she has even been compelled to work a low-paying job that she squeezes in when the children are at day care. This situation is causing stress and trouble for me and my husband: We always thought our midlife years would be a time when we could travel, spend time together without the problems caused by young children in the house, and so on. Now we find ourselves baby-sitting and caring for our grandchildren. We love our daughter and grandchildren very much, but we are forced to wonder whether we are doing what's right for her and her children. What do experts think?

PROFESSIONAL OPINIONS

Sharon J. Price, Ph.D., Researcher and Professor, University of Georgia; Past President, National Council on Family Relations

This is a challenging situation but an example of the contributions families can make in times of stress or crises (i.e., "this is what families do"). There are several things, however, that I would suggest. First, the parents and their daughter should discuss if there are, in reality, any alternatives to the present situation. (I would guess the daughter is not any happier with the present situation than are her parents.) Open communication could foster a more relaxed atmosphere and fewer feelings of exploitation. I assume the parents would not want their daughter to return to an alcoholic and abusive spouse; therefore, there may be no alternatives at this time. Given this fact, strategies should be jointly developed to increase the daughter's independence, with the goal of her and her children living in their own home. For example, if the parents can afford to help her financially or if there are other sources of income available through community agencies, this move may take place sooner rather than later. In the meantime, all efforts should be made for the daughter to obtain extra job training and/or education, which would aid her in securing a better-paying position, thereby contributing to her independence. Extra efforts at this time may result in a more satisfying solution in the future.

Robin J. H. Russell, Ph.D., Author, Researcher, and Faculty Member, University of London

～ Is your concern totally what is right for your daughter and grandchildren? You sound to me as if you are more put out by not leading the sort of relaxed life you have been looking forward to. If you really are concerned about the well-being of your daughter and her children, keep up the support. She really needs it right now. But don't be too tough on yourselves either, or you will end up resenting her. So sit down with her, discuss the situation, don't hide any of your feelings, and draw up some ground rules regarding what you are prepared to do for her and what you expect her to do for herself. Good luck, and, if you feel you are being asked to sacrifice too much, ask yourself why you chose to have children! Despite the drawbacks at times like this, I'll bet you don't regret it.

BOTTOM LINE

➤ Both experts come down on the side of helping the daughter and grandchildren—"this is what families do" in times of crisis. The woman in this situation needs to ask herself these two bottom-line questions: (1) Am I more interested in being a helpful, supportive parent to my newly divorced daughter and her children in their time of need? Or (2) Am I more bent on enjoying the fruits of the long labor that my husband and I have endured? There are no ways around this analysis. Either she decides to continue helping out her daughter and grandchildren, aware that doing so comes at a cost—such as the unhappy possibility that she and her husband could drop dead suddenly and never get to enjoy the travels they worked so hard for. Or she decides to tell her daughter and grandchildren that they must find another solution but that she is still willing to contribute financial support to the extent that it does not interfere with her travel plans or desire to spend time at home alone.

Another question worth asking is whether the daughter knew this man was an alcoholic before she married him, or whether she married him against her parents' wishes. If so, her parents may feel like she made her bed and now must sleep in it by coping on her own. It can be tough to want to sacrifice for someone who knowingly entered into an abusive relationship. The bottom line is that this woman should be open and explicit in her communications with her daughter so that there are no silent but deadly unfulfilled expectations.

It's very difficult to run an army if the general
is in love with the sergeant.
    —Margaret Mead

        Happiness depends, as Nature shows,
        Less on exterior things, than most suppose.
                    —William Cowper

After the game, the king and pawn go into the same box.
    —Italian proverb

Problem 57

I AM A THIRTY-TWO-YEAR-OLD UNMARRIED woman with a demanding career as a physician. I have had trouble meeting nice guys through my profession—all the men I have met have seemed too aggressive and too caught up in their work. Last month I hired a carpenter to renovate a room in my house, and I have found myself becoming increasingly attracted to him. He is basically uneducated, but he is a kind and decent person. My friends and parents have warned me not to get involved with him—they said that ultimately we will find we come from different worlds and that we have little in common. But I find myself being drawn to him, and his desire to marry and have a family appeals to me. What should I do?

PROFESSIONAL OPINIONS

Gregory D. Morrow, Ph.D., Author, Researcher, and Associate Professor, Edinboro University of Pennsylvania

➤ You seem to be seeking some assurance that this relationship will "work" before you pursue it further. However, if you do become involved with this individual, no one can tell you how the relationship may evolve. Why do you have such concerns about becoming involved with a man whom you are attracted to and whom you describe as kind and decent? Perhaps you are uncomfortable with the "reversal" of gender roles that this relationship presents.

If you do become involved with this man, you will be in a position of having more education, a greater income, and more social status than your partner. While it is admirable that you recognize these differences exist, should they stop you from pursuing what might be a very rewarding relationship? Would you be concerned if his education, income, and so forth exceeded yours? Since you are attracted to this man, I suspect that the two of you share some important similarities. I would encourage you to pursue the relationship, but given your reservations, perhaps you should do so slowly. Instead of focusing on his desire to marry and have a family, maybe you should start by meeting him for coffee or dinner.

Judith Worell, Ph.D., Author, Researcher, and Professor, University of Kentucky; President, Division of Psychology of Women, American Psychological Association

➤ Many professional women I have known experience a similar challenge in finding a man of their own education and income level who is willing to establish an egalitarian relationship. It seems that you are seeking warmth and caring and wish to avoid a competitive situation. This relationship can work, providing you understand and accept what it can offer you, as well as its limitations. If the young man is also interested, you both should discuss openly your attraction and reservations about a potential relationship.

Then, try seeing each other for a while. If you are enjoying each other's company, consider how you might spend your shared time. Do you have sufficient interests in common, and are you each willing to engage in the other's activities? Of equal importance, how will each of you deal with the income disparity? Will you feel resentful when you contribute a larger share to joint expenses? Will he become resentful of your earning power and the status of your profession? For some, income represents power and the right to make family decisions. If these critical issues are explored and resolved to the satisfaction of both, you may have found your man.

Randolph R. Cornelius, Ph.D., Author, Researcher, and Associate Professor, Vassar College

➤ Your friends and parents are correct in some ways in their thinking that you and he are from different worlds. You are. There is no way around the fact that your education and social status make you different. However, the fact that you are attracted to him, and presumably he to you, indicates that you probably do have something in common. Similarity of opinions, values, and ways of seeing the world has been found to be a powerful predictor of who will be attracted to whom, so my guess is that you are attracted to one another because you sense at least the possibility that you share something significant. Relationships, however, are not only discoveries, they are creations, and part of what goes on in a new relationship is creating ways in which you and your partner are compatible.

Before you get much more involved with this man, however, I would suggest that you reflect on what it is that you value in him. Since our emotions are based on how we appraise or assign value to the people and events we encounter, thinking about our emotional responses to the world can reveal to us how we see the world and what we value in it. Use your attraction to this man to learn a little bit about yourself. If you find that your emotional responses to him are based on something that you value highly (having a family, for example), and that the value you place on this is higher than the value you place on having a mate whose profession is similar to yours, by all means proceed with the relationship. With a little creativity, it is entirely possible to overcome your differences.

BOTTOM LINE

～All the experts agree that there are potential risks in pursuing this relationship but that it can succeed. The bottom line is that this woman should move slowly with this man. If they do a few things together without getting heavily involved too soon, she may discover that her attraction to him is based more on what she wants him to be than on what he actually is. But she may also learn the converse: that he is the perfect antidote for the stress of her career life. Over a few months of friendly involvement, the woman can watch how this man handles the fact that she is a doctor and is from a higher socioeconomic level than he. Perhaps his background was similar to hers (as children), and perhaps they followed different trajectories for different reasons. Thus, they may have more things in common than one might suspect from their occupations. He may be completely happy with what he does and who he is, in which case the relationship could work out well. Or he could end up being envious and feeling resentful of her success. Time will tell.

But allowing herself to fall madly in love is not a good idea, at least not before the data are in. In the first few weeks of an attraction, people sometimes do stupid things. One other aspect she should attend to immediately is having this man complete all his work for her, paying him promptly, and ending this aspect of their relationship. It is unwise to start spending lots of time together or dating while one individual is employed by the other.

Beware of the man who praises women's liberation;
he is about to quit his job.
　　—Erica Jong

Most women would rather cuddle a baby than a typewriter.
　　　　　　—Phyllis Schlafly

Work and love—these are the basics. Without them there is neurosis.
　　—Theodor Reik

Problem 58

I WANT TO QUIT MY JOB AND be a full-time mom after our first child is born, but my husband says we cannot afford the loss of my income. The sacrifices are worth it as far as I'm concerned, but my husband says that we will have to sell one of our cars and that we won't be able to travel or even have enough money for clothes. He says the baby will do fine in day care, and he points out that most children are placed in day care. The trouble is that my job is extremely demanding and I don't believe I can handle my job and a baby. Plus, I am exhausted from working these past eight years, and I would welcome the opportunity to stay home and care for our family and house. What should I do?

PROFESSIONAL OPINIONS

Jay Belsky, Ph.D., Author, Editor, Researcher, and Professor,
Pennsylvania State University

➤ Quit your job and stay home with your baby. In view of the fact that you are unlikely to be happy being away from your baby while you work, and will in all likelihood find yourself stressed out at the end of the day when you can be with him, it is doubtful that letting someone else take care of your child is in either his or your best interest. Add to this the fact that high-quality infant care is more the exception than the rule, especially when one does not have lots of money to spend on such care, and it becomes ever more likely that, from your baby's perspective, it makes lots of sense for you to assume the role of full-time mother.

Of course this means that you will have to deal with your displeased husband, who clearly does not prefer this solution. You should point out to him that by the time one covers the costs of going to work (transportation, food, clothes) and paying for child care, it is unlikely that there will be much real additional income from your job to contribute to the family budget. Make it clear to him, as well, that family life will likely be much less stressful if one of you can devote yourself full-time to the home and the child, rather than having to force so much into evenings and weekends. Finally, be sure to write your representatives in local, state, and federal government to push for tax benefits for families like your own who are rearing the next generation. Good luck.

Frieder R. Lang, Ph.D., Author and Researcher, Free University of Berlin

◣ I can understand that this is a serious dilemma for you. It is difficult for me to give you any valid advice without knowing more about your long-term plans and goals. I don't know how old you are, but it seems that there are still many opportunities ahead of you. It seems that you have now reached a turning point in your life. Your goal is to become a good and caring mother, and you think you need a lot of time to master this task. It seems natural that this goal involves the necessity to give up on other aspects of your life. Becoming a parent and educating a child is a lifelong commitment that entails rapidly changing tasks for you and your husband, as well as your child.

It seems important to consider that your child will benefit from parents who have achieved their life goals. You may also want to consider your husband's part. Do you want him to be actively involved in the father role? Will he be happy as a full-time working father with having only a small amount of time for his family and a lower living standard than he feels comfortable with? If your plans are to reenter the job market in a few years, this will be less difficult if you keep in touch with your profession, for example, on a part-time basis. This way you could contribute to your family's income as well as find time to be a good mum for your child.

BOTTOM LINE

➤ This couple has many issues to consider and debate, and it might be best to work through these issues with the help of a marriage counselor. On the one hand, the man may feel that he and his wife each promised to bring home half of the bacon, and that now she wants to renege on her commitment to be an equal partner. He himself might be happy to give up a stressful job—or to work part-time—in order to care for the baby, and he might resent the implication that it is always the woman who is allowed to stay home with a child. The wife, on the other hand, may feel that she has pushed herself at her job for eight years, and has undergone a tiring pregnancy while working, and that she is due a break. She may deeply wish to stay home and raise her child, and she may believe that in exchange for the physical and emotional work involved in having a child, her husband owes her nothing less than supporting her and making the necessary sacrifices to live on one income.

First, this couple should lay out their entire financial situation and compute exactly what they earn and what they spend, and exactly what they would have if she quit her job—remembering the lower tax rate that would apply, her lower expenses given that she no longer buys special clothes and lunches out, the fact that no child care would be required, and so on. Next, the couple should ask what type of lifestyle they would have without the wife's income. If they sold their newer cars and bought a couple of older cars, for example, would this help lower monthly debt?

Finally, as the experts pointed out, the couple should discuss alternatives, such as the wife taking six months to a year off, then changing to a less stressful job or even a part-time job. Equivalently, the man should be allowed to register his desire—if applicable—to work at a less stressful or part-time job and take on child care responsibilities. Perhaps a limited amount of day care could be combined with part-time work by one partner and full-time work by the other. In sum, this woman should realize that it may be her overstressed work environment that has turned her off to the idea of working in general. There are many jobs that would be less stressful and would occupy fewer hours. In addition, this woman must accept the fact that it is not her husband's responsibility to support her but rather that her husband and she have equal responsibilities to support the family. Perhaps, once the child is six months to a year old, both partners can establish careers that leave them time for child care, and both can make equivalent sacrifices.

When you meet a gent paying all kinds of rent
for a flat that would flatten the Taj Mahal,
Call it sad, call it funny, but it's better than even money
that the guy's only doing it for some doll.
—Lorenz Hart and Richard Rodgers

Take back your mink, take back your pearls.
What made you think that I was one of those girls?
—Lorenz Hart and Richard Rodgers

Problem 59

WHEN I MET PHILIPPE THREE YEARS AGO, it was like winning a lottery. He was handsome, suave, and rich, and he really knew how to show a girl a good time. He cut a dashing figure with his bright white teeth, bronze skin, and wavy chestnut hair, which blew in the wind as he drove around town in his red Mercedes 380 SL convertible. He bought me candy and flowers on each date and took me to the finest restaurants. He was forty-seven (or so he claimed), and I was thirty-nine. All my friends were envious because the single guys in our town are usually gay, psychos, liars, or losers who are still carrying a torch for some woman who dumped them a decade ago. As time went by, however, I started to wonder if Philippe was all he claimed. Once he got his way with me, the flowers and candy stopped. And the only time he takes me to a restaurant now is when he has a two-for-one coupon for a free meal (plus all the salad and rolls you can eat). He even expects me to pay for my half of the bill!

Recently, I discovered from an old high school friend of Philippe's that he's an impostor: The Mercedes is leased, his teeth are fake, his hair is a weave, and his sole source of income is stuffing mailboxes with advertising flyers when his own car (a 1981 Yugo) is running. I learned that Philippe's real name is Harvey, that he's sixty-two years old instead of forty-seven, and that he has a wife and three grown children in Hoboken, New Jersey, which he fled to avoid gambling debts. When I confronted him with these accusations, he readily admitted they were true, and apologized for misleading me. He said he was so in love with me that he'd do anything to impress me. Last night Philippe (Harvey) told me he wanted to marry me. He said I was the only woman he ever loved, and that he could not imagine life without me. If I were the skeptical type, I'd wonder if his proposal was related to his discovery that I will soon inherit a large sum of money when my father, who is very feeble, passes away. All my mother keeps saying is, "So what if he's sixty-two? You're no spring chicken yourself, my little fatty. You could do a lot worse!" Am I overreacting by worrying? Is life with Philippe (Harvey) better than being alone?

PROFESSIONAL OPINIONS

Stephen J. Ceci, Ph.D., Author, Editor, Researcher, and Professor, Cornell University; President, Division of General Psychology, American Psychological Association

➤ Psychologists have known since the 1920s that nearly everyone lies at least some of the time and under some conditions. Rather than simply complaining about others' deceptions, one should try to analyze the conditions that prompted a person to lie. According to your description, Hoboken Harvey has engaged in lies at three levels, which are not equally serious. At the most extreme level, it is very serious when a man withholds the truth about having a wife and kids. Even if this were his only act of deception, it might still be enough for you to tell him to get lost. On the other end of the deception spectrum, I am somewhat less bothered by Hoboken Harvey's cosmetic deceptions (false teeth and hair weave), because these are signs of low self-esteem. The goal of these cosmetic deceptions is not to lie per se but rather to elevate one's self-esteem. This doesn't make it right to mislead someone about one's appearance, but this is a very different type of dishonesty than lying about a wife and children in another city.

Lying about his age or about owning a Mercedes 380 SL (which he leases by the day, no doubt!) falls somewhere in the middle. These are rather pathetic attempts by Harvey to bolster his image in your eyes. I find it sad that he feels he needs to do this to impress you. Instead of suggesting that you chastise him for this behavior, however, I first want to know if you are the type of woman who *is* impressed by such superficialities. If you are, you deserve to be deceived! (Note that I am completely unsympathetic to your complaint that Harvey takes you to cheap restaurants and no longer romances you with candy and flowers: At least he takes you somewhere. I didn't hear you say you ever took him anywhere or bought him flowers, despite your greater wealth—or did I miss something?)

Given that Harvey lied about his age, you have two options: You can dump him and start searching for a younger man, if his age is important to you. Or you can ask yourself (and Harvey) why he felt the need to lie about his age in the first place. It sounds like there are not many available guys in your town who will start bellying up to your trough if you give Harvey his walking papers. As your own mother says, "You're no spring chicken yourself." If I were you, I'd ask myself if I really saw something in this guy to love (you never say you love him, by the way, and this may be revealing). If your answer to this question is yes, I would cut him some slack. Okay, he owns a ratty 1981 Yugo, and he stuffs flyers in mailboxes for a living: This shows he's willing to hold down an honest job. Why not ask yourself how you'd feel about Harvey if he had been up front about his false teeth and hair? Would you have rejected him? This guy takes pride in his svelte, bronzed appearance, and some women would be grateful he's not some geriatric slug. How would you feel if a man rejected you upon discovering you'd had a face lift or liposuction or colored your hair? The question is not simply "Did Harvey lie to me?" but rather "*Why* did he feel the need to lie to me?"

Obviously, Hoboken Harvey is no gem, but at least he's trying to impress you. Your mother knows both of you far better than I do, and she appears to believe that even without his hair, teeth, and money, Harvey is a worthy catch for you. However, just because your mother thinks you're no day at the beach doesn't mean Hoboken Harvey represents your last or best chance for lifelong companionship. Only you can evaluate the odds that someone better will walk into your life the minute you dump Harvey. Until you make up your mind about this, quit being so materialistic and stop judging this flawed but possibly salvageable man in terms of his ability to wine and dine you and squire you around in a fancy car. In view of your younger age and greater income, you might even try bringing *him* flowers and candy and helping with his paper route!

Wendy M. Williams, Ph.D., Author, Editor, Researcher, and Associate Professor, Cornell University; Recipient of the 1996 Early Career Award from the American Psychological Association

⚓ Ditch the bastard! Better yet, turn him in to the authorities—he probably owes back alimony and child support. Why would you want to have anything to do with this chiseler? He's a thieving weasel who doesn't deserve you. And as for your mother, if she loves him so much, tell her to date him—after all, they're the same age! What's wrong with the name Harvey anyway? Does this guy have a love affair with the French or something—where did he get this Philippe thing? Plus, do you want to end up riding around in a car you have to roll-start? Next thing you know, you'll be pushing while he pops the clutch. I don't care if you're "no day at the beach"—you deserve better than some weasel who lives an assumed life. Dump him now, before your father kicks the bucket and you inherit all the cash, lest your dear Philippe sweet-talk you out of a portion of your inheritance—or even steal it outright.

BOTTOM LINE

~ There seems to be some disagreement between these two experts, perhaps originating in the life experiences and expectations of members of different genders. One expert refers to Philippe/Harvey as a "flawed but possibly salvageable" man, while the other terms him a "chiseler" and a "thieving weasel." The questioner herself seems unsure of how to proceed with Harvey's offer of marriage, especially given his knowledge of her impending wealth. Perhaps (as a first step) the questioner could determine whether Harvey is legally divorced. (The up side here is that Harvey might not be able to marry the questioner to get her inheritance—he might not even be divorced!) If he is, the next question is whether his personal debts are on or off the scale. A wise woman might also investigate Harvey's whereabouts during any long absences, since he might have other women (or children) in his life as well. The questioner's skepticism shows that there are many causes for alarm. Thus, a wait-and-see attitude is clearly warranted in this case. Her mother might be right—she could do a lot worse—but she could also do a lot better, even if she winds up alone.

Epilogue

THE TWELVE GOLDEN RULES
OF PERSONAL DECISION MAKING

IN THESE FINAL PAGES, we share a dozen important rules to keep in mind when thinking through personal problems. Each of these rules is drawn from many years of experience and wisdom on the part of decision-making experts. Failure to keep these rules in mind can ambush even the most sincere attempts to advise ourselves and others.

1. There are two or more sides to every story.
There is an old saying among lawyers: "If you've been told only one side of a story, you know less than half of it." Throughout this book you have read one-sided accounts. Each person wrote about a problem, but only from her or his own perspective. What if we asked their spouses or children for their "takes" on these problems? Do you think the spouse or children would agree with the way the writer framed the problem? We doubt it. They'd probably argue that the writer had distorted facts and omitted important details.

This is a risk we are rarely told about when we listen to media gurus answer their callers' questions. Throughout this book, experts occasionally questioned the validity of the way a problem was framed. Similarly, when listening to media relationship gurus or friends we should always ask ourselves how a person's partner would react to the way the person framed the question. Would the partner agree that the situation is exactly as the person has described it? Sometimes the same problem, when posed from another's perspective, turns out to arouse quite different sympathies in listeners.

A case in point is the way problem 12 is framed. Note that this writer complained that his wife refused to wear sexy underwear and engage in oral sex. Based on the way he framed the scenario, his wife emerged as the main problem. She denied him the pleasures he had come to expect—ones which are neither deviant nor painful and which many ordinary adults engage in. Now take a look at problem 36. See the difference? It's the same situation, but from the wife's perspective. Note that she does not use phrases like "sexy underwear" but rather "sleazy evening apparel," and she complains of being forced to perform acts she finds personally demeaning or insulting to women. Who is right depends to a great extent on which framing of the question you accept as closer to reality.

The same is true of problems 1 and 17. Here we have a man (problem 1) and a woman (problem 17) who are in committed relationships. When their old flames contact them, they are torn, in part wanting to honor the commitments made to their partners, but in part wanting to pursue the exciting new possibilities. Again, these are flip sides of the same situation, and you might try asking yourself whether you reacted differently to the two sides because of the way the questions were framed. Similarly, problem 15 and problem 54 address opposite sides of the same situation, as do problem 6 and problem 51. The world of relationship problems is strewn with alternative framings; there are *at least* two sides to every story. As psychologists, we rarely hear a question posed by one partner that is accepted by the other as accurate. It is one of the hardest rules to learn when solving personal relationship problems, but it is the most important: Always ask how the other side might challenge and reframe the same "facts." Failure to follow this rule means you know less than half the story. The bottom line is, don't be sucked in by the way someone frames a problem until you've heard the other side.

～ 2. Always seek a second (or third) opinion.

This extends rule 1 to the realm of advice seeking. Most of us know that if we were told we needed a serious medical procedure, like major surgery, we would immediately seek a second opinion. For example, if we were told that we needed to have a limb removed to prevent the spread of an infection, we would go immediately to another physician to get an additional judgment. Yet when it comes to psychological opinions, we are not sophisticated consumers of advice. We seldom seek the view of a second, independent mental health professional. This is unfortunate because, as you have seen throughout this book, psychological experts sometimes disagree with each other, even dramatically! People change jobs, lovers, or child-rearing styles because some expert advised them to, without getting another equally qualified expert's advice. Sometimes they would have been advised by a second expert to stick with the present job or lover.

No single professional has cornered the market on wisdom. The bottom line is that you should not settle for a single professional's viewpoint if a lot is at stake: Get a second (or even third) opinion before making a life-altering decision. Doing this can be inconvenient and expensive, but you owe yourself nothing less. Your life will be easier and cheaper in the long run.

～ 3. The truth usually rests somewhere in the middle.

Many of us crave certainty. We are fed up with advice that seems to fence-sit by striking a balance between a strong opinion in our favor and one that is equally strong against us. No one wants to receive wishy-washy advice. This is why media relationship gurus have become so popular; they are willing to advocate solutions clearly, unequivocally, and without hesitation. But there is a hidden danger in craving advice that rejects

218 Wendy Williams and Stephen Ceci

a compromise. Most problems are not cut and dry, and do not lend themselves to strong, one-sided opinions.

George Bernard Shaw remarked: "The pure and simple truth is seldom pure and never simple." Shaw's insight is important to bear in mind whenever we want someone to give us strong advice. Many times strong advice will be wrong for the simple reason that people are more complex than the slogans that often constitute strong advice (such as "Never marry out of your religious faith," "Never consider abortion," and "Divorce is not an option"). Few situations are entirely one-sided, and, consequently, few solutions should be. Beware of those who claim to possess the pure and simple truth.

 4. When in doubt, sleep on it.
Countless errors in decision making could be avoided if only people did not rush to judgment. While it is natural to want closure on a problem, and the impulse to resolve a troubling situation is understandable, it is important to take time before leaping to a decision. Sometimes the best thing we can do is to do nothing. Sleep on it. Many times the problem will seem different or less pressing after waiting awhile. If you doubt this fact, try visiting the local courthouse and asking defendants, if they had it to do over again, what they would do differently. Many of them would say that they acted impulsively, out of anger or fear. In hindsight, the perceived insults or threats that spurred their criminal behavior have faded; in hindsight, they wish they had slept on it before acting.

The same could be said for some relationship disasters we have observed. The boyfriend of one woman was out running errands on the other side of town when he saw his girlfriend leaving a motel with a good-looking man. The two were laughing and had their arms around one another. In a fit of pique, the boyfriend went to the apartment he and his girlfriend shared, packed his things, and left a scathing note condemning her infidelity. The next day he learned the man his girlfriend was with was her cousin, who had come to town unexpectedly on a business trip, and called her and asked her to meet him for lunch. The boyfriend felt like an idiot. He also looked like an idiot, because he had acted like an idiot. His girlfriend doubted his grip on reality. The moral? Don't rush to judgment—things are not always what they seem. If you *assume*, you often make an ass of yourself.

⬛ 5. If you're too close to a problem, it can be difficult to see a solution.

Remember problem 17, about the woman who was in a committed dating relationship with a man she loved, but when a man from her past showed up she found herself mysteriously drawn to him and wanting to date him? This woman's problem had less to do with dating her old flame than with the status of her current relationship—even though she framed the problem in terms of whether she should date the man from her past. This woman was so close to the situation that she could not see this rather obvious point.

This is one of the most valuable services an expert can provide, an impartial analysis. At times such objectivity can cause us anger because our closeness to the situation "blinds" us from seeing alternative views. We want an expert to validate our feelings, not challenge them. Often, however, some emotional and psychological distance can help us by bringing a solution into sharper focus.

⬛ 6. Not everyone shares the goal of solving the problem.

Some people who get involved in helping resolve our problems are invested in *prolonging* rather than solving our problems. This can be one of the hardest realizations to arrive at. We have a colleague who is known for inserting herself into other people's problems, then developing grand schemes to solve them. She has a vested interest in seeing that the problems do *not* get solved satisfactorily: Her goal is to make the individuals rely on her for emotional support. So whenever a solution to a problem is inconsistent with her effort to make someone rely on her, she will misdirect the individual. She "stirs" people's fears and resentments because by doing so she replaces their other friends, often presenting herself as their one true advocate. Beware of false friends who try to convince you that your problems are worse than they may be, or that these false friends alone are your saviors! And watch out for anyone who tries to convince you that extreme actions are needed when your own instincts tell you the problem is not dire.

━ 7. Beware the advice of "disinterested parties."

This rule is related to number 6, but goes beyond it in scope. Many times we need to ask ourselves what agenda someone has before we accept her or his advice as gospel. For instance, one well-known radio personality has a moral objection to abortion. Because of this objection, she denounces any caller's consideration of abortion as a solution to a relationship problem. This expert does not always tell callers she is opposed to abortion on moral grounds. Instead, she cites psychological studies to dissuade women from choosing abortion. However, psychological data could be cited to support virtually any decision regarding abortion—it just depends on which data and studies one chooses to cite!

All experts can be expected to have personal, moral, and political agendas, and it is appropriate for us to keep this in mind when we weigh the advice they give. This does not invalidate their advice, of course, but it does alert us to the need to consider other options if our own moral agendas do not coincide with the experts'.

━ 8. Dependency is the enemy of objectivity.

We both know a woman who for years was financially dependent on the man she lived with. So enmeshed were her physical and emotional needs with her financial needs that she could not see how toxic this man was, to both her and her daughter. As a general rule, the more you rely on someone for your primary physical, emotional, and financial needs, the less likely you will be to see this person for what he or she is. If you sense that you may be overly dependent on a person, seek advice from someone outside your relationship, preferably someone who knows both of you well. Dependency is an integral aspect of intimacy, but it can go too far and become unhealthy. You need to be vigilant about maintaining an open mind and a clear perspective regarding your own dependencies, otherwise excessive dependency may cloud your analysis of any situation.

~ *9. Recognize the repetition rut.*

Have you ever wondered why we always seem to date—or even marry and remarry—the same kinds of people? One of the wisest insights in the field of personal problem solving is that we tend to repeat the same mistakes, re-creating past problems in different guises. Edna St. Vincent Millay remarked: "It is not true that life is one damn thing after another—it's one damned thing over and over."

In the 1960s a series of famous psychological experiments demonstrated what is known as learned helplessness. This work showed that sometimes an animal with a history of being held in an abusive environment (for example, being given inescapable electric shocks) would later fail to escape abuse even though it was possible to do so. The animal had come to learn that there was nothing to be gained by trying to escape, so it would lie on the cage floor and passively accept its fate. People who are in abusive or alcoholic relationships have been likened to such animals. They have histories of repeating the same mistake, always getting involved with the same kinds of losers. In essence, they fail to recognize they are in a repetition rut. The moral? Don't be one of these people.

~ *10. Two wrongs don't make a right.*

When we detect that someone has been unkind to us, we may want to retaliate immediately and relentlessly. This is a natural instinct. But the adage "two wrongs do not make a right" should guide us. Not only is retaliation morally wrong, it belittles us because it announces to the world our willingness to stoop to dirty tricks to get even. Divorce courts are full of parties who can correctly recall callous deeds by their partners, often carried out in response to misdeeds by their partners. But those judging us will not view our misdeeds as justified just because they were in response to even more heinous misdeeds. We must remember how we will appear to others when we, too, engage in dirty tricks. Sometimes the most dignified and smart reaction is to walk away.

➤ *11. Keep it simple, stupid (KISS).*
Don't be seduced by jargon or by complicated analyses. Sometimes the best insight into a problem is the first one that strikes us, and efforts to complicate our analyses are not likely to result in better decision making. Some of the most profoundly important insights have been the simplest to arrive at. A case in point is when someone's partner has a fundamental character flaw: say the person is a child abuser or substance abuser, or a philanderer. The obvious solution is for the individual to leave this partner, take the child out of harm's way, or whatever. But some self-help books are filled with complicated analyses, such as "the person needs familial support while going through therapy in order to improve." These analyses can short-circuit good decision making by needlessly clouding a straightforward picture. Often the first solution is the correct one, and the complex considerations are merely obfuscations.

➤ *12. You are the one and only expert on your own life.*
By now you know our view of expert advice: The goal of this advice is to provide you with analyses of the factors that are relevant to your problem. This is a valuable service for the reasons already mentioned; namely, we are often too close to a situation to see it clearly and/or we are too immersed in emo-

tionality to be objective. But experts cannot fully direct your decision making: Only you can do this. You must view expert advice the same way a business owner views a consultant hired to analyze a problem. The consultant is trained to think about problems differently than laypeople do, and to apply expert knowledge about underlying factors that laypeople may not possess.

But it is up to us to take what the experts reveal to us and place it in the context of our lives. No expert can do this for us. We acknowledge the value of expert identification and analysis of factors that are pertinent to each situation. However, we believe that no expert can decide for us how much weight to place on each relevant factor, because no expert knows more than we do about the contexts of our lives. With this point in mind, we end at the beginning, with Cicero's time-tested dictum: "Nobody can give you wiser advice than yourself."

Authors' Note

Dear Reader,

Do you or someone you know have a relationship or child-rearing question that you would like the experts to answer? If you send us a short description of your question, we will consider using it in a future volume.

Please omit or change any information that identifies you or anyone else. Send your question by E-mail to jmm30@cornell.edu (on the subject line type "Advice Trap"), or by U.S. mail to Wendy M. Williams and Stephen J. Ceci, Department of Human Development, Cornell University, Ithaca, NY 14853.